Endo

I have known Ken Gaub both as a friend and spiritual leader for many years. He is always "real," and a tremendous man of faith. His unique approach will challenge you to live a practical Christian life. His positive faith in God and humor will endear him while he is teaching you how to live victoriously and effectively for Christ. Ken is a tremendous soul-winner wherever he goes — on planes, in restaurants, and on the street. I know that this book will be a great blessing as you read and apply it to your own life.

— Paul Fisher, Walled Lake, MI; pastor, educator, Assemblies of God district presbyter

What you read in this book exemplifies the real Ken Gaub on a daily basis. When he walks in and speaks, the room lights up. I have seen him in action many times. What he teaches really works.

— Quentin Edwards, Dallas, TX; pastor, evangelist, missionary-evangelist

I highly recommend the ministry of Ken Gaub. His ministry builds up the body of Christ with God's Word and with faith and joy. My faith is stirred by being around him. He challenges my vision to grow. You will enjoy this book.

— Jack Holt, Kent, WA; pastor of River of Life Fellowship

I enjoy time with Ken, my friend and travel companion of many years, because Ken's mind is

like the eagle he loves. It soars above life's obstacles. Fresh, positive ideas flow from his mind as easily as snow falls in the mountains of his Washington. This book will help you spread your wings of faith and soar on the winds of God's power.

— Dale Carpenter, Yakima, WA; pastor Stone Church, camp meeting speaker, Assemblies of God district presbyter, Ken Gaub's pastor and friend

Sky High Faith

20 Success Secrets for Making Your Faith Produce Results

Sky High Faith

20 Success Secrets for Making Your Faith Produce Results

Ken Gaub

New Leaf Press

First printing: June 1995
Second printing: May 1997

Copyright © 1995 by New Leaf Press. All rights reserved. Printed in the United States of America. No part of this book may be used or reproduced in any manner whatsoever without written permission of the publisher except in the case of brief quotations in articles and reviews. For information write: New Leaf Press, Inc., P.O. Box 726, Green Forest, AR 72638.

ISBN: 0-89221-295-0
Library of Congress: 95-69893

Note: This book contains quotes by a number of people. The use of a quote does not mean a blanket endorsement of all their views or their lives by this author.

All Scripture references are from the King James Version unless otherwise noted.

Dedicated to:

My Board Members:

Dale Carpenter
Robert Foreman
Bill Haldeman
Mel Hurst
Dan Wold
John Gaub
Dan Gaub

. . . who believe in this ministry and continue to help in every way possible. And also to other friends God has placed in our lives to pray, support, and sow seed, so that many around the world will hear the gospel and turn to Christ. Over the years a giant harvest has turned to Christ. Thank you so much.

Special thanks to JIM and CONNIE AGARD who always spoke in a positive manner to me, had faith in me, encouraged me, and said,"YOU CAN MAKE IT!"

List of people who are quoted or otherwise mentioned in order of their appearance (Bible characters not included):

Secret 1
Corrie ten Boom
Arne Anderson
Jack Holt
Dave R. Williams
Tim Dudley
Abraham Lincoln
Cal Carpenter
Dale Carpenter
Vern Knox
Ron Stevens
Paul Fisher
E.W. Kenyon
Billy Joe Daugherty
Bob Morehead
Secret 2
Jeff Farmer
H.L. Hunt
Dale Carpenter
Jim Marocco
Billy Graham
Charles "Tremendous"
    Jones
Secret 3
Dale Carpenter
Don Lyon
Oral Roberts
George Bush
Don Lyon
Margaret Thatcher
Don Lyon
Secret 4
Smith Wigglesworth
John Gaub
Charles Capps
Shirley Ericson
Frederick K.C. Price
Smith Wigglesworth
John G. Lake
T.L. Osborne
Secret 5
Gloria Copeland
Herschel Gammill
Dan Wold
Roy Hicks
Dean Lunsford
Bill Cosby
Helen Keller

Calvin Coolidge
Secret 6
Becki Segura
John Avanzini
Robert Schuller
Jim Agard
Henry Kaiser
Kenneth Broadus
Rich Wilkerson
Henry Ford
Dexter Yager
Secret 7
Paul Harvey
Quentin Edwards
Secret 8
Sam Smucker
Dave Williams
"Woody" Clark
Secret 9
Monty Hipp
Secret 10
Jim Whittaker
Herschel Gammill
E.W. Kenyon
A.W. Tozer
Paul Fisher
Rod Parsley
Jim Agard
J. Don George
Quentin Edwards
Secret 11
Dave R. Williams
Dexter Yager
Richard Roberts
Dexter Yager
Randall Ross
John Lloyd
Secret 12
Kenneth E. Hagin
Dr. David Yonggi Cho
Jim Menke
W.H. Heaston
Jerry Savelle
Dan Wold
Tom Watson
Secret 13
Fred A. Manske Jr.
Rosalynn Carter

John & Hellen
    Barnes
Harvey Mackay
Secret 14
Marilyn Hickey
H. Norman
    Schwarzkopf
Jim Agard
Don Meares
Secret 15
Carl Allen
Dan Gaub
Henry Ford
Secret 16
Jannessa Gaub
Theodore Roosevelt
John Maxwell
Robert Schuller
Abraham Lincoln
Secret 17
Connie Agard
Helen Keller
Daisy Osborne
Billy Joe Daugherty
Winston Churchill
Smith Wigglesworth
Secret 18
Charles Capps
Woodrow Yasuhara
Dr. Paul E. Paino
Don Lyon
Rich Wilkerson
Secret 19
Dwight D. Eisenhower
Erma Bombeck
Charles "Tremendous"
    Jones
Jim Agard
Connie Agard
Dave R. Williams
George W. Cecil
Robert Townsend
Secret 20
Chet Allen
Virginia Nordberg

Contents

Foreword

It is my pleasure to introduce Ken Gaub's latest book, *Sky High Faith,* for your reading pleasure. You will quickly find that the book contains a wealth of positive, faith-building hope.

On a weekly basis, I speak to thousands of people of all backgrounds. Be they well-to-do or at the bottom of life's economic strata, many of them talk to me about the "grind of life." The constant pressure of just trying to keep a family together, food on the table, bills paid, and a semblance of romance in a weary marriage is draining.

If you knew Ken, you would know a man who has practiced every principle in this book. He has a wonderful family, three grown children, and five grandchildren. Ken has built a worldwide organization from Yakima, a small town in what most of America considers the mysterious and barren great Northwest.

Ken has never met a stranger in his life — everybody likes him! I can't tell you how many times through the years I've walked onto a United Airline flight from Seattle to Chicago to hear all the passengers in First Class laughing and find Ken at the center of it all. If you know him well, you love him.

How has this man fought and won in the "daily grind"? You're getting ready to find out. Read on!
— Rich Wilkerson

Preface

How exciting it would be if everything you wanted happened exactly the way you wanted it. Anyone who succeeds at anything in life must first recognize the causes of failure. You can take any challenge or crisis you have faced and turn it into a steppingstone if you want to. No one can make you angry, force you to be afraid, or cause you to fail without your full consent and cooperation.

Be an optimist. An optimist is a man who falls out of a 20-story building. As he passes the tenth floor, he says, "So far, so good."

Don't be a pessimist. That's a person who feels bad when he feels good, because he's afraid he'll feel worse if he ever gets better.

This book, if used wisely, can help you:

- Recognize new opportunities
- Acquire "unbeatable thinking"
- Get your hopes up
- Cultivate creative vision
- Have a correct image of how big God is, and what He can do
- Think accurately
- Reach your goals

Some don't succeed, because they only *learn* principles and don't really apply them. *Apply* the principles you learn, and with God's help you will succeed.

— Ken Gaub

Secret 1

FAITH — That Produces Results

We are going to talk about faith, what it is, and how it works. You probably bought this book because you want your tomorrows to be better than your yesterdays; your future more blessed than your history.

I will do my best to tell you what some of my experiences have been, what I have learned, and what God has shown me. You may be thinking, *Although it works for others, will it work for me? What is my role?*

> *Faith is the radar that sees through the fog. — Corrie ten Boom*

During much of my ministry, our operations

required that we own and operate some large vehicles, both trucks and buses.

Years ago, while driving through the hills of Idaho with an old tractor trailer which had vacuum-boost brakes, we started down a 12-mile grade. This piece of road had a bad reputation because the grade was not only long and steep, it also contained some hazardous curves.

"Arne, don't you think 70 is a little too fast?" I asked the driver. Looking at his face, I could see that he was tense and nervous.

"I know, Ken," he said, "but I've been trying to slow down. The brakes are gone."

"Well, gear it down," I instructed, trying to stay calm.

He slammed in the clutch and strained at the gearshift. "It won't budge!" he yelled.

I tried to help him, but it was impossible to disengage the gears. He pulled the emergency brake, and I looked back to see smoke billowing from between the dual wheels, but we didn't slow down.

"Ken, I'm scared! You take over!" he pleaded.

By this time the speedometer registered 80 miles an hour. I yelled, "Let me have it!"

As stupid and dangerous as it was, we quickly maneuvered so that Arne slid under me as I grabbed the wheel and we traded places. The needle continued to climb. Arnie prepared to jump. "Don't do that," I pleaded, "you'll be killed at this speed."

Several times the trailer tried to jackknife as we rounded the curves. As we neared the bottom of the mountain, still building speed, we rounded a corner to find a Greyhound bus a short distance ahead.

Instantly, the thought passed through my mind, *If I don't try to pass, I'll hit him in the rear end, and we'll all be killed. If I do pass, and a car is coming, we'll all be killed. I have to try it.* "God, please help us all," I prayed aloud.

As I maneuvered around the bus at 90 miles per hour, the passengers and driver stared in what seemed to be utter disbelief. The truck was vibrating so badly that we feared that it would shake apart. The tires literally screamed.

Soon, the road leveled out. We coasted for some distance before we were able to stop at a wide spot along the road. Arne Anderson and I got out of that cab on very unsteady legs to walk around and examine the truck and trailer for signs of damage. We thanked God that we were still alive. As the Greyhound passed us, the driver honked loudly and shook his head.

God had definitely spared us. Our initial mistake had been not gearing down at the top of the grade, but God had overridden our ignorance. We had to trust Him, and promised not to repeat our mistake the next time.

> *Faith, without God's anointing, will not work. — Jack Holt*

Faith means staying in the guidelines that God has set for us in His Word. Hebrews 11:6 states: "But without faith it is impossible to please him, for he that cometh unto God must believe." We must first believe that He exists, and second, that He rewards those who diligently and sincerely seek Him. You can never please God without faith.

The eleventh chapter of Hebrews has been called God's Hall of Fame for Men of Faith. The chapter says that they all obtained a "good report" through faith. If you want a good report (and we all do) you can only have it through faith.

"Faith is the substance of things hoped for, the evidence of things not seen" (Heb. 11:1). Do you carry a picture in your billfold of someone who is not with you? That picture is evidence that this person exists. Along with your word, it is the evidence that this person really is.

Faith is the evidence, the substance, the photo. It's the reality of things we cannot see. Faith will change your hopes into something that will become reality.

> *Faith is seeing things that others absolutely cannot see.*
> *— Dave Williams*

When we really believe God's Word, we will stand on that Word without question. Real faith, when we think about how it works and what it will produce, will challenge your life. It will cause you to believe that answers to your needs can become a reality. It will help put God's energy and miracles to work in your life.

> *Faith is the courage to keep going forward, when everyone else is telling us to stop.* — *Tim Dudley*

During an extremely critical time of the Civil War, Abraham Lincoln wrote to a friend, "I am profitably engaged in reading the Bible. Take all of this Book upon reason that you can, and the balance upon faith, and you will live and die a better man."

Perhaps he meant that most of the Bible can be taken upon reason and only a small part requires the use of faith, but if you accept the Bible as a revelation from God, all of it must be taken by faith.

Faith is the only force in the entire universe that can cause the invisible to become visible. When a building is built, somebody had to have material. It didn't pop up one day by accident.

This book didn't just happen. Years of experience and evaluation came first. There were hours of discussion with my pastor, my dad, and other friends. Then came more long hours of compiling, writing pages of notes, editing, rewriting, and lots of prayer. Finally, the process necessary for the actual publishing and printing preceded the existence of the volume in your hand. From the very start, I visualized the finished product, and knew it could help people to exercise faith.

The only place success comes before work is in the dictionary.

Only God can take what is not there and cause it to exist. With just a clap of His hands, a snap of His fingers, or a spoken word. He said, "Let there be light," and the lights were on. When God speaks, something is going to happen. If you let Him, He will speak into your life.

> *Faith is the key that can turn your biggest problems into your greatest victories.* — *Cal Carpenter*

Some people, when faced with misfortune, believe they are doomed to bad luck. (I personally don't believe in "luck," good or bad.) Negative emotions take over.

We should not become discouraged when we fail. Let your faith in God be so strong that success overcomes your failure. Faith can be the starting point that will lift us out of negativism and other destructive forces.

Real faith is not based just on theory. It is not based just on doctrine. It is not based on denominational creed. It is not based on a theological supposition. In order to succeed and survive, to stand the test of time, in order to be a positive force in a negative world, to resist all the tides of fear in our negative society, real faith has to be based on that which is infallible and impregnable. The foundation of real faith can't be shaken or disputed, because it is the Bible, the Word of God.

Only that kind of faith can accomplish miracles in lives. My pastor, Dale Carpenter, says that faith is believing God doesn't lie. He will do what He has promised to do.

I love the Word of God, and I believe that I

can trust it. You can't trust everything. In this world, many things will let you down. Anything that endures must be built on truth and trust. If it isn't, it will lead down a path of misery, failure, and poverty, and end in death.

> *To me, faith is just holding on until you see the promise fulfilled. —*
> *Vern Knox*

I trust my parents, but when I was a kid, I learned not to trust my mother to comb my hair when she was upset with Dad. In high school, I really didn't trust my shop teacher: he had three fingers missing. You wouldn't trust a sleepy pilot, a lawyer who is in jail, or a dog that is foaming at the mouth.

You must use your faith, your belief that God can make things happen. Abraham Lincoln failed time after time. But he always picked himself up and tried again. It seemed that he would never succeed, but in his mind of faith, he was a winner. God used him to help save our nation.

Sometimes, we learn things quickly, but the hard way. A blacksmith was fixing a horseshoe. He heated it on his forge, took tongs and hammer and shaped it, then immersed it in cold water and threw it in the sand. The owner of the horse, not realizing that it was still hot, picked it up to examine it. He quickly dropped it.

"Is it hot?" the blacksmith asked.

"No," answered the man, "it just doesn't take

me long to look over a horseshoe!"

Some people imagine things. Faith is not imagination, but faith has imagination. Sometimes suggestions can spark our imagination. Imagination comes from the word "image," which means to paint a picture. Without imagination, knowledge is devoid of life.

It has been said that whatever the mind can conceive can be achieved. Great inventors, musicians, writers, and leaders became great because they had creative imaginations.

If you want to build a home, can your mind imagine it now? Do you dream about it? When you start dreaming about it, put it down on paper; your imagination will take the intangible and a picture is painted. Plans form, and you are on your way. Ideas are a product of your imagination. History records the dreams which had imagination.

Once your mind is stretched by a tremendous adventure of faith, it will never again return to its original shape.

> *Faith is the arm of the soul that reaches forth to God and never returns empty.*
> — *Ron Stevens*

Unbelief is taking sides against God. We don't have faith for the things which we can see and touch. We decide to believe or disbelieve things which we are told, but cannot see. You can see this book. If I tell you that I have written several others, and you have not seen or read them, you have to believe that what I say is or isn't true. Faith then enters into the picture.

Faith is believing without any proof whatsoever. Faith is believing something you can't see. God doesn't trick us. He is saying, without any proof other than His Word, "I am big enough to meet your need, if you will just believe that I am bigger than your need, I will take care of you."

Stop floating through life hoping for some kind of break. Put your faith in God, He is your opportunity, He is your break.

We sometimes argue with God. We acknowledge that He made the universe. However, we seem to think that our need is too big for Him, when in reality, it's just small peanuts for God. You can survive discouragement, disappointment, setbacks, temporary defeats, and other challenges. The God of this universe wants to help you.

> *Faith is like super glue, it binds you to the living God. — Paul Fisher*

We should stop and think. God didn't send Jesus into this world just to get us from hell into heaven, He sent Jesus into this world to get himself out of heaven into us. God is a big God.

Hebrews 11:3 says, "Through faith we understand." You have to use faith to understand many of the things in the spiritual realm. You also need faith for many things in the world around us.

I don't really understand how an airplane can

fly. Looking at a giant 747, my natural mind says, "No way. How could that thing, which weighs tons, possibly rise to the altitude of 40,000-plus feet?" But because I have flown in airplanes, I am willing to board another one and trust that it can do the same thing.

> *When the spirit is in perfect fellowship with the Lord, faith is as natural as breathing.*
> — *E.W. Kenyon*

People watch us to see if our faith is what we claim it is. James remarked that "Some one will say . . . show me your faith" (James 2:18;NKJV). The things we do are the way we show our faith.

I use lights and vacuum cleaners even though I don't fully understand the principles of electricity. When I turn on the switch (my faith), both of these work for me.

Living their faith is the reason that some are working tirelessly to help the homeless on the streets of our cities. That's where a cardboard box is the only shelter against the elements, and what few belongings they possess are bundled up under their arm, or used as a pillow as they cover up with a piece of cardboard. It's where people scavenge through dumpsters for bits of food and clothing that they hoard in cast-off shopping carts.

The love that faith generates causes people to forget the safety and comfort of their own homes. It causes them to take food, blankets, and comfort to those who are broken and alienated from their family and friends.

God can go no farther than our belief in Him allows. Living by faith is a way of life. It's a way to understand the things that happen around and to us.

I have always had a hard time understanding "flash floods." We travel along the area of the Dead Sea, and see signs along dry creek beds telling us not to cross if water is present. My reaction has always been, "That's a silly sign. How could the little bit of water that comes through here be dangerous?"

Then one day, as we traveled toward Masada, there was a large truck laying on its side several yards to the downstream side of the road. Just a small trickle of water now flowed under the road.

I looked at our bus driver. "What happened?" I asked.

"Yesterday," he told me, "we could not have crossed here. The water overflowed the road. It was not extremely deep, only two or three feet, but it was very powerful. That driver ignored the signs and see what happened."

> *Faith is in the present tense; it believes now, it receives now, and it acts now.*
> — *Billy Joe Daugherty*

"By faith" Abraham took a leap into the unknown, leaving the security of Ur. But it was not a blind, stupid, foolish leap. God doesn't ask us to take foolish leaps. God had spoken to him, even though Abraham did not know what to expect.

God gave Abraham some general dreams and directions. The exact specifics of how it would all come together were as unknown as the bottom of the ocean. He obeyed God and waited patiently for the answer to come.

Many of us have faced difficult and trying hardships and felt as if we were at the bottom of an ocean, even though we knew that God had called us to a specific job. Any "leap of faith," like Abraham's, involves scary risks at times.

We often have to leave our "comfort zone" and move into the realm of the previously unknown. That can make us feel like we are walking a tight-rope without a safety net.

> *God commands me to run through a brick wall. It's my job to run, it's His job to make the hole.*
> — *Bob Morehead*

We're always sure that we have more than we can take care of; we forget what God can do. Sometimes, we have an incorrect image of who God is, and what He actually can do.

It's not the greatness of my faith that moves mountains, but my faith in the greatness of God.

Faith is an essential ingredient and God has it arranged so that we can believe Him. We should never pray for faith; we have faith. Why pray for something we already have? Paul wrote in Romans

12:3, "Dealt to every man the measure of faith."

Talking about faith is not the same as acting on it. We can talk for weeks about planting a garden, but until we get the shovel and some seeds, all that is going to grow is the weeds.

You have faith. So let's talk about what you know, and what you do with what you know. Knowledge alone doesn't guarantee success. It takes putting theories and plans to practical use to be successful.

Some teach finances, but have none of their own. It's foolish to take financial advice from someone who can't control their own finances. Some handle a lot of money, but are also broke. They teach certain things but don't use the knowledge of what they teach.

You can acquire all the knowledge necessary to become a missionary, but unless you go to the mission field, you won't be a missionary.

We have faith, so we need to exercise the faith we have. As we exercise our faith for small things, it grows. It becomes easier and easier to exercise our faith for bigger needs.

> *The first secret is: You have the faith to produce results you need.*

Secret 2

FAITH — Your Thinking

A bulletin board for a church displayed the following quote:

> You are not what you think
> you are, but you are what you think.
> "As he thinketh in his heart, so is he"
> (Prov. 23:7).

In this world which is so full of pretense, deep down in our heart of hearts is where we really find out who we are. The way you walk and talk, dress and carry yourself, all reflect the way you think.

It is amazing how many problems could be solved if we would just use some common sense and think. We often try a lot of things, because thinking seems to be so hard to do. We react instead of thinking. I once watched a bullfight on television. The bull reacted to the red cape; the matador did the thinking. Consequently, the matador won.

Faith will also help you develop quality thinking. Nothing around you — not your job, your family, nor your problems — makes you what you are. The way you think about those things, and react to them, makes you what you are.

> *Faith is the coin of heaven; it is the kingdom currency for every divine initiative. — Jeff Farmer*

As we get ready to board the jet on our overseas trips, we say to those traveling with us, "If you don't have faith to fly over the ocean, you don't need it. The rest of us have it. (We don't say that braggingly.) I've crossed both the Atlantic and Pacific Oceans dozens of times, and if you don't have the faith to cross the ocean in a jet, you don't need it. I've got people of faith with me, and we have the faith." We pray for God's protection. There are often others who hear us and ask that we also pray for their flight, which, of course, we do.

Our thinking controls our believing and our believing controls how we talk. It becomes a cycle; we can get caught up in the wrong thing. Faith will help break a negative cycle and develop the quality thinking that the Bible teaches. It's a refreshing feeling to think positively. If you're lost in a sea of confusion, thinking *I can make it safely to shore*, can help you succeed. If you panic and don't believe you can make it, you probably won't.

Many times, it is how you think about or consider a situation. Someone reported to billionaire H.L. Hunt, "Your son is losing a million dollars a year, what do you think of that?"

Mr. Hunt hardly looked up from his desk as he replied, "Wow, at that rate, he'll be broke in about 500 years."

Negative thinking can never produce positive results. Eliminate negative thoughts immediately and replace them with positive ones. The moment negative thoughts hit you, recall the good things God has blessed you with, and know that what He has done He will do again.

To understand a problem, first look at how it developed, then start thinking differently. Start thinking answers instead of problems. Start looking for possible solutions instead of dwelling on just the problem and letting it get you down. There are some who are almost as good at creating problems as they are at solving them.

> *Faith is the hope of help on the way. — Dale Carpenter*

Many people who have come from a background of poverty feel that God wants us poor.

Thinking correctly can help overcome limitations, activate your world, and get you over higher hurdles. Start thinking that God wants us to be blessed materially so that we in turn can bless others. As I have often said, your life moves in the direction of your most dominant thoughts.

A beggar accosted a man on the street. "Would you give me $2.00 for a sandwich?" he asked.

The man retorted, "Not until I see the sandwich!"

> *The secret of getting a miracle is to get close to God.* — *Jim Marocco*

Tim was voted "Least Likely to Succeed" in his high school class. He didn't manage to graduate until he was 25. When he went to his 10-year reunion, everyone wanted to see him, because they had heard he had become a multi-millionaire. He arrived in a long black limousine. They crowded around him and asked what had caused his success. He replied, "Well, I bought stuff for $1.00 and sold it for $4.00. That 3 percent profit made me a lot of money!"

Many potentially successful futures, possibly happy marriages, and probably fruitful lives have been hijacked by wrong thinking.

Have you ever noticed that for those who think, bigger and bigger things happen? Maybe this should tell us something. "Trust in the Lord with all your heart; never rely on what you think you know" (Prov. 3:5;Good News).

Many things in this world will try to rob our

minds of their positive influences. Negative attitudes and people are the worst bandits. It seems easier for our minds to be taken over by negative thoughts than by those which are positive. We need motivation and frequent reinforcement by mental images of success.

A minister discovered at the last minute that he had forgotten to invite one little lady to the church picnic. He called at the last minute and asked her to come. Her reply was, "It's no use, I've already prayed for rain."

> One with God is a majority.
> — Billy Graham

A classified ad said: WANTED, 16-year-old boy to work in an office. Twenty-five boys arrived for interviews. The boy in the back of the line thought, *There is no way to be first in this line, so I'll think ahead of the rest.* He wrote a note and slipped it to the secretary; telling her, "Please give this to your boss, I'll tip you later." The note read: "I'm the 25th boy in line. Don't hire anyone until you have a chance to talk to me. I'm your man."

He got the job.

We need to think ahead, even if we are in the back of the line. You can reach any goal if you think accurately, and your mind is programmed by God. We need to keep in mind where we are going, what our goals are, and what we want to achieve.

You were born to win, you were created to

succeed by God. Always remember that God has and is the answer; there is nothing too hard for God.

Faith puts energy to work and helps overcome obstacles. It actually removes many limitations.

> *You are the same today that you are going to be five years from now except for two things: the people with whom you associate, and the books you read.*
> *— Charles "Tremendous" Jones*

The story is told that a large American shoe manufacturer sent two salesmen to Africa. They were supposed to open the market there. The company received a telegram from each of the salesmen.

The first telegram read, "I'm coming home. No one wears shoes in this country."

The other salesman had written, "What an opportunity! No one has shoes. Send many pairs of every color and size as soon as possible. The market is unlimited."

As you raise the quality of your thinking, you will learn to be creative in witnessing to others about the Lord. You can help your church grow if your thinking is right. God has a plan for your life which may be much greater than you now think.

Our thinking will be changed as we read God's Word and cooperate with the Holy Spirit. Paul told the Philippians to think about things that were true, noble, just, pure, lovely, of good report, and praiseworthy (Phil. 4:8).

Your thinking can help make you a success or a failure. Your thoughts can free you or imprison you, help or hurt you. Your thoughts control the way you react to situations; they make you laugh or cry, love or hate.

Think about helping. Think about giving. God is our faithful source. Look around for people to bless. The more we give to Him and to others in His name, the more God gives back to us. And don't forget, He has a bigger shovel.

> *Secret number two: Change your thinking to look for solutions.*

Secret 3

FAITH — Your Mind

When God gives you a thought, that's a fax from God. My God-given fax machine runs overtime. The fax in our office had to be turned on, connected to a telephone line, and have paper in it before it could begin to receive a fax (now, it's always on).

Before you can use this book successfully, your mind must also be prepared to receive. An open mind is usually a mind that has been set free. If you close your mind, you are locking out possible miracles.

> *Faxes from God are the real facts.*
> *— Dale Carpenter*

We can't control a lot of things — a tooth-ache, the loss of our hair, or the "character lines" as we age. Our minds are something that God has given us control over. Our minds were given to us by God, and they are ours. We are the boss, so to speak.

It has been said that you can't keep the birds from flying over your head, but you can keep them from building nests in your hair. We can't keep negative thoughts from coming into our mind, but we can refuse to dwell on them. We can't always control circumstances, but we can control our reaction to what happens to us. Our mind controls our attitude.

> *What looks like trouble is really faith on its way to greatness.*
> *— Don Lyon*

We need to fill our minds with the positive so that there is no room for the negative.

The story is told that a certain moonshiner was set free from alcohol. He decided that the only way to be sure that he didn't "backslide" was to just stay home. Eventually, he had to go to the store for groceries. On his way, it was necessary to pass both a tavern and a small cafe. The cafe had a sign in the window advertising, "ALL THE BUTTER-MILK YOU CAN DRINK, 25 CENTS."

He promptly went in and drank 10 glasses of buttermilk. As he continued past the tavern, some-one heard him say, "Devil, I'm so full of buttermilk that there's no room for anything else!" Of course, the answer is not to get full of buttermilk, but to get full of God's Word.

> *The important thing is not the size of your faith, it is the One behind your faith: God himself.*
> *— Oral Roberts*

As I discussed in the book *Dreams, Plans and Goals*, our brain is a very complex computer. It contains approximately 100 billion nerve cells which begin to die from the time we are born. These tiny cells perform like power plants, generating their own electrical power. They also produce hundreds of chemicals that affect how we react to situations, and our moods.

The brain also has a housecleaning system with vacuum cleaner cells which collect dead and injured tissue, depositing it into the nearest vein to be carried away by the blood stream.

There are basically three major parts to the brain: the conscious, the subconscious, and the autonomic. The subconscious stores all the data that we seldom use, and is guided by the conscious. The autonomic controls your body functions, digestion, heartbeat, breathing, and other involuntary actions.

Our mind cannot be physically seen or touched. It is the computer software program written on our brain. It's a billion dollar gift from God. We draw our conclusions from the material fed into the program. Unlike many computer programs, our mind has the ability to draw more than one set of conclusions from each situation.

The conclusions we come to determine our attitude, which in turn determines whether we choose to react in a negative or positive manner in any given situation.

> *Use power to help people. For we are given power not to advance our own purposes nor to make a great show in the world, nor a name. There is but one just use of power, and it is to serve people.*
> — *George Bush*

The mind is a storage facility. Always remember that whatever you put into your conscious mind is going to affect both your thinking and your behavior.

Computer memory is information stored on hard disks, where we leave the files we use frequently; or floppy disks, where we transfer files we don't need very often. We store information in our memory, either conscious, where it is easily reached, or subconscious, where it may take a bit longer to get to. (We could liken the operating program to our autonomic system.)

A computer operator can decide that any part (or all) of the information on the disk(s) is no longer desired, and with a few simple keystrokes, can remove it and start again. It takes God's power to do this to our mind.

When God renews our mind through the power of His Word, we can conquer all the negativism that Satan throws our way. Our negative past, our past failures, our negative thoughts and desires can all be conquered. We no longer need to allow the devil to control our lives, and beat us up for past mistakes, failures, and actions.

We need every area of our lives renewed. Satan will know that Christ is in you and your mind is renewed. Have the mind of Christ. It will put you in the "I can do it," "We can make it," "It will happen," class of life.

> And be not conformed to this world: but be ye transformed by the renewing of your mind, that ye may prove what *is* that good, and acceptable, and perfect, will of God (Rom. 12:2).

That's one reason we should be very careful in our choice of the material we put into our minds. We need to discipline our television viewing. "Soaps," whether daytime or primetime, can create a lot of marital dissatisfaction. It's hard for your mate to measure up to some fantasy person you saw on TV. There are much more edifying choices of material with which to fill our minds.

We also need to monitor the materials which our children and grandchildren feed into their minds. Thoughts become words, words become actions, actions become character, and character affects our destiny. In order to have faith work in our life, we need to control the input into this very sophisticated computer that God gave us, called the mind. Learn to separate truth from supposition.

You may have a great idea that you've thought about for a long time, but you really haven't acted on it. You haven't moved in that direction. You have every quality that it takes to succeed, if you will only put the plan into action. It will require discipline, and faith in your abilities.

Maybe you are lacking in self-confidence. Find something that you are interested in and learn all you can about it. Read about it. Become an expert, an authority on this one thing. It doesn't have to be something big or complicated, maybe just a single bird or flower. It will build your confidence for other things as well.

Your success or failure may be entirely a matter of how you discipline your mind. If you have never done this, it may not be easy at first. The mind can rebel at any type of discipline. It seems to like its own way, rather like a spoiled child.

No wonder the Bible says to think about the things that are clean, pure, true, and honest. If we really want to succeed, we have to rid our minds of negative thinking. It takes putting a rein on our thinking, rather like bridling a horse.

> *The sun doesn't rise to observe your faith, but it may rise in someone's heart because of it.* — *Don Lyon*

Maybe you are thinking that if you are a

success, your ego will get carried away. The ego itself is not a bad thing. However, some egos are so weak and lacking in courage that they can keep you paralyzed with indecision. Others are badly over-inflated. There is a balance.

Maybe you think that a Christian is not supposed to have an ego. Ego is actually another term for our inner self, our will. Psalm 27:1 says, "The Lord is my life and my salvation; whom shall I fear? the Lord is the strength of my life; of whom shall I be afraid?"

As children, most of us learned the story of David and Goliath (1 Sam. 17). Goliath challenged the men of Israel to send someone to fight him. Because he was more than nine feet tall, no one dared to accept the challenge. David, who was probably still in his teens, had brought food to his brothers, who were in the army.

David couldn't stand to hear Goliath's mocking. He went to King Saul and told him, "I will fight this Philistine. God helped me kill both a lion and a bear, when they were after my sheep. God will also help me slay this giant who is defying the army of the living God."

Then David said directly to Goliath, "You come to me with a sword, with a spear, and with a javelin. But I come to you in the name of the Lord of hosts, the God of the armies of Israel, whom you have defied. This day the Lord will deliver you into my hand, and I will strike you and take your head from you. . . . That all the earth may know that there is a God in Israel" (1 Sam. 17:45-46;NKJV).

What an ego! But David balanced his claims

with confidence and faith in God.

It can be a disaster if your ego weakens. Your ego is the seed of your willpower, and must be fed in order to remain healthy. When your inner self is wounded, your will to go on can be hurt or destroyed. Many of life's failures are because of a weak or indecisive will.

We know that within each of us is the God-given force called the will. Properly used, with determination and purpose, this force is capable of overcoming unbelievable obstacles, breaking barriers, and washing away opposition.

A strong, clean motive is essential. Your motive and desire to accomplish things will help your ego, which should be valued and protected like any other precious possession. Don't let others pollute it with thoughts of fear and problems. Don't fill your mind with negative thoughts, — assassinate them.

Self-discipline strengthens your mind. You don't have true self-discipline until you organize your mind and keep it clean of bad influences. Every principle of success has to function through your mind. Keeping your mind orderly is a controlling factor in the process of becoming successful.

> *Being in power is like being a lady, if you have to tell people you are, you aren't. — Margaret Thatcher*

One division of the mind transcends all others by unbelievable odds; the power of the will, or ego. The power of the will is almost limitless. It may be said that the only limitation which you have is the one which you place on yourself, by limiting the use of willpower.

Faith is more than a state of mind. The way you use your faith is by instructions from your inner man. You draw from the knowledge that God can help you. You fill your mind with all the information you can find related to your subject and with positive attitudes.

The promises of God can make you know you have the things you desire. You have to some way convince your inner self that you believe you will receive that for which you are asking. We do this again and again by constantly introducing our mind to the promises of God that assure us we have that thing that we are believing for. This is not "new age." It's Bible. I hate new age ideas, but I love God's Word.

> *The world won't laugh at you, once your faith works. — Don Lyon*

How you perceive a situation is important. It can determine how you feel, what you think you can do, and even what your future will be.

Keep your mind free for what God can and will accomplish in your life. It will help you realize there is no problem that can't be solved, no mountain that can't be climbed. It will get you off of the side road of fear and onto the highway of faith.

Once you get the inner man convinced, it

will cause you to act upon what you really believe. Then you will begin to make a definite plan to get what you desire. In other words, the Holy Spirit will give these to you, and you won't have to worry about it; He will give you an answer.

> If you abide in me, and my
> words abide in you, ye shall ask what
> ye will, and it shall be done unto
> you"(John 15:7).

Jesus told us, "Greater is he that is in you than he that is in the world." The willpower is so great that it is known to stay the hand of death in some cases. There are no shortcuts, and control of the will comes with a high price tag. The price is applying these principles correctly and understanding that with a pure faith you have a definite purpose to achieve your goals. You won't fear any challenge or situation.

Anyone who sells his principles for popularity will become bankrupt. Some will use willpower for greed. God will not bless this desire. You must be forgiving and loving, and not envious. Manage your mind and don't let it get out of control and take you down a negative path.

> *Secret number three: Fill your mind with positive input so you can receive from God positive results.*

Secret 4

FAITH — Your Believing

The first step in accomplishing the impossible is to refuse to believe that it's impossible.

Some people are so negative, they probably go to the dog track and bet on the rabbit. They might pick up a seashell, put it to their ear, and get a busy tone.

> *I am not moved by what I see, I am not moved by what I feel, I am only moved by what I believe.*
> *— Smith Wigglesworth*

Many years ago, when we were just starting in the ministry, my wife and I were in Colorado, on our way from Kentucky to Idaho and

Washington. This was before credit cards were in common use; we had no bank account, and we were out of cash. Actually, I think we had one dime. (We may not have been "broke," but we were badly "bent.")

It was winter, and our oldest was still a baby. We pulled the car beside the road and bowed our heads in prayer, asking God to supply our needs for fuel and food. After we finished praying, we drove to a nearby gas station. The attendant came to the car and I asked him to fill it with regular. I truly believed that I would have the money to pay him by the time he finished.

> *Faith is knowing God, and what you want from God, and not just sitting there, but acting on your faith.* — *John Gaub*

As he began filling the tank, another car drove in. A lady got out and walked over to our car. She told me that as she and her husband were leaving the grocery store a few blocks down the street, they noticed a car with Kentucky license plates. They remarked that it looked as if the passengers were praying. She told me that they felt we had a financial need, and as her husband was writing out a check, we drove away. They followed us to the station, and gave us a check for $25. She told me to fill in my name, the station would cash it.

About that time the station attendant came

to my window. He gladly accepted the check, and gave us the change. In those days, when gas cost less than 20 cents a gallon, we had enough money for gas and food all the way to Idaho.

> *There is no need to pray the problem, what you need to do is zero in on the answer. Speak the answer, cast the problem over on Him.* — *Charles Capps*

A town in England had been bombed heavily during World War II. When the workers were clearing away the debris, they found a Prayer Book, open to Psalm 27, and verse 13 was marked. "I had fainted, unless I had believed to see the goodness of the Lord in the land of the living."

The incident was reported and widely commented on, and was believed by many to be at least partially responsible for the high morale which the British maintained in spite of the intense bombing raids which Hitler carried out. This level of faith in God, as much as the military might of the Allies, is credited for the ultimate defeat of the Axis powers.

Faith is not believing that God can, but simply believing that God will. There is power in believing in God that will give you drive, enthusiasm, and confidence. It will help you accomplish and eliminate frustration, negativism, and self-pity. It is almost a forgotten virtue.

We believe that certain things that we do

will cause other things to happen. When I was a boy, my sister Shirley was chasing me around the house one day. My dad asked her why she was chasing me. "Because he punched me," was her reply.

Dad asked me why I had punched her. My answer was, "So she would chase me."

God does not bless every kind of believing. There is a believing that God will bless; the example is found in John 20:24-29.

Some of the disciples had seen Jesus raised from the dead, and they reported it. There was a problem — Thomas didn't believe it. He said basically, "I won't believe that unless I see it for myself."

Jesus walked into the room, and said, "Thomas, touch My hands and My side. Don't be so skeptical, but believe." Thomas responded, "My Lord and My God!"

Jesus said, "Thomas, because you have seen, you have believed, but blessed are they which have not seen, and yet have believed."

> *You can believe all day long that the Bible is true — and that's to your credit — but what the Bible says will never affect your life in a personal way until you start acting on God's Word.*
> — *Frederick K.C. Price*

God blesses those who believe without actually seeing. It's important that you don't doubt. There will be times when things don't seem to be working out right. If you look at the circumstances, you will begin to doubt. This is a tool of Satan.

When I teach on goals, people tell me about their obstacles. Any road that leads to accomplishment always has obstacles. We're in a constant process of change in our lives. In every adversity there is an equivalent seed of success. To every disadvantage, there is an advantage. I work like everything depends on me, but believe like it all depends on God. Everyone with ambition wants to move forward.

Romans 8:28 reads, "All things work together for good to them that love God." Notice that it doesn't say that all things are good. Even bad things work for good in the life of the child of God.

> *I can get more out of God by believing Him for one minute than by shouting at Him all night.*
> *— Smith Wigglesworth*

You may have a lot of problems. Read the Bible. Jesus said, "These things have I spoken unto you, that in me ye might have peace. In the world ye shall have tribulation: but be of good cheer; I have overcome the world" (John 16:33).

The word tribulation could also be translated pressure or problems. As long as we are in this world, we will face problems and pressures. Be happy, your problems don't have to be catastrophes or disasters. You can believe and expect God to give you a miracle. Acknowledge the challenges, but let God bring you through them.

> *It is not our long prayers but our believing that gets the answer.*
> — *John G. Lake*

Our ministry began as what would be considered a "home missions" pastorate in the mountains of Kentucky. But we had no missions board or organization backing us with even minimal support. We depended on God's working in the hearts and wallets of our friends and family. Many times, when we wrote to thank my parents for amounts of $20 or $50, my father would write back to scold me for not keeping my books straight. "I only sent $5 (or $10), not the larger amount," he would chide.

We still believe that God must have changed the amount of the currency (it was never checks) between Washington and Kentucky. God knew what the need was, and supplied it as we believed Him.

> *A doubter often prays for things he already possesses.* — *T.L. Osborne* *(Eph. 1:3)*

Our believing must be balanced by God's Word. He has promised to supply our needs, to give us good things, and even to provide the desires of our hearts, when our hearts are "perfect" toward Him. He has not obligated himself to give us frivolous desires, sinful pleasures, or those things which will draw us away from serving Him.

Paul wrote, "My God shall supply all your needs" (Phil. 4:19). James warned, "You ask and don't receive, because you ask amiss, that you may spend it on your pleasures" (James 4:3;NKJV).

It's sometimes hard to stay balanced when we want the front seat of the bus, the back pew of the church, and the middle of the road.

Jesus told us, "What things soever ye desire, when ye pray, believe that ye receive them, and ye shall have them" (Mark 11:24). Activate your believing.

> *Secret number four: Believe for the impossible and act like it's accomplished.*

Secret 5

FAITH — Your Attitude

Attitude is very important to faith. Life is 10 percent what actually happens to you, and 90 percent how you react to it. Faith in God will help you create a proper attitude in your life. It will create the attitude and good spirit that are needed for your faith to operate.

> *Prayer does not cause faith to work, faith causes prayer to work*
> *— Gloria Copeland*

Faith and a good attitude are Siamese twins. One will always be found with the other. They are inseparable. Faith is the power locked in you; your attitude controls the action to unlock it.

I was seated on a plane; a lady with a baby was trying to get settled beside me. The baby was crying, and the mother was trying to get her bag kicked under the seat, while trying to stop the baby's cries. I said, "Lady, hold it. If you'll stop hitting him, he'll stop crying." (I learned this when I was a child, because I started out as one.)

"Let me hold the baby until you get the bag under the seat," I continued. "I don't know who you are, but since we're going to be sitting together for 12 hours, you aren't going to have that kind of attitude and sit by me. But I believe that inside you is a wonderful attitude, and I want to help you. We'll take turns with the baby, and work together and become friends."

She smiled and said, "Okay," so I took the baby and was holding and patting him. I kept talking about how positive my attitude was, how I teach on attitude, and also have books, tapes, and videos on attitude.

About that time, the baby threw up all over me. What a mess! Try to get cleaned up in an airplane restroom — it's not easy. But I managed to keep my attitude straight, at least on the outside. After my remarks to her, I had to.

> *Faith is the difference between a success and a failure.*
> — *Herschel Gammill*

Faith and attitude work together. Faith will put you on the building crew. When you find people who are constantly finding fault with everything, they're on the wrecking crew. They need to get on the building crew. Noah, Abraham, Jacob, Joseph, Moses, and the other men of faith in Hebrews 11 were all on the building crew.

Noah built the ark by faith, when it had never rained. Abraham's life of faith is so notable that he is called the "father of the faithful." Isaac, Jacob, and Joseph all believed God's promise, but didn't live to see it fulfilled.

Moses' mother hid him for three months, even though Pharaoh had decreed that all baby boys were to die. Moses' faith accomplished mighty acts when he led the Israelites out of Egypt.

If your attitude is right, it will help you have balance to your faith. This is very important. God is sensible, practical and well-balanced. I preach faith and believe in creative speaking, but I know that God gave us brains. God, our ultimate example, is sensible, practical, and well-balanced. We should also strive to follow His example.

> *Faith keeps my heart rejoicing no matter what attacks my life.*
> *— Dan Wold*

Jesus didn't teach us to deny the existence of problems. He didn't tell us to say we're not sick when we are. There's a balance. You can't deny a broken bone. If it's broken, you have two choices: pray and ask God for healing and see it happen, or have a cast put on it.

> *God's attitude is very plainly stated, He is a God of compassion and healing. Believe it and act upon it. —Roy Hicks (3 John 2)*

God gave us brains. A friend of mine ran out of gas. His comment was "Just like the devil!" I told him the devil had nothing to do with it. He could blame him if he wanted, but the solution was to put gas in the car. Using common sense would have solved the problem.

Jesus knew sickness would be real, so He let them lay those stripes on His back. "By His stripes we are healed." Otherwise, the stripes would have been useless. He didn't teach us to deny our illness.

Faith will even help you remain in charge of your behavior during a crisis, large or small. One test of faith is having the ability to recognize a challenge before it becomes an emergency.

I was driving in a strange city when a man pulled out in front of me and I had to brake hard to avoid him. I hit my horn loud and long (maybe a full minute.) He shook his fist at me. In a few blocks, we both had to stop for a light, next to each other. We glared at each other.

Then I realized that my attitude was definitely not right, my spirit softened, and I mouthed "I'm sorry," and smiled. He rolled his window down, so I did, too.

"I'm sorry, too, I shouldn't have been driving like that," he said.

Now, I knew that (that's why I had honked so long), but I accepted his apology. "You want to hear something funny?" he added. "I'm a Christian."

I grinned, "Want to hear something funnier than that? So am I!" As we both laughed, we heard horns behind us honking and looked at the light just in time to watch it turn from yellow back to red. Now we were affecting the drivers behind us. So understand that your attitude is important. It can even affect the attitude of those around you.

> *If we are going to move mountains, we need a little faith in a great God. — Dean Lunsford*

I've told millions of people: There's no such thing as a hopeless situation, but people can grow hopeless about their situation. Even if you fail 999 times, count each failure as practice. When you finally succeed, just once, you win. You made it happen because you didn't give up. A good attitude helps you keep going.

Sometimes our planning needs to change so that basic structures are right. Then the thing we are building will have a proper foundation. Part of the right structure is a proper attitude.

God is a big God. People sometimes give up just before God would have answered their prayer and worked a miracle. I love people who don't give up even though they have handicaps and difficulties. They can smile and live above them. You don't stub your toe standing still. It's when you move that the chance of stubbing your toe increases, but the chance of getting somewhere also increases.

We do not have a dead spirit living inside of us, but a living spirit.

You can't steal second base while you keep one foot on first. You have to move on, doing what is absolutely necessary, which becomes possible. Sometimes you even accomplish the impossible.

Choose to be a positive person. Have a positive attitude. Faith and a good attitude will help you change your world.

A dead fish floating downstream needs no energy. A fish swimming up the river requires a lot of energy. You can change your world with energy, direction, dedication, commitment, purpose, and a good attitude.

We have the ability, through faith in God, to change our attitude. We're not responsible for others, only for ourselves. We have the ability to reason, to go beyond the impossible, and reach altitudes of answered prayer.

The circumstances which separate failure from success are often so slight that the real cause can be easily missed.

> *I don't know the key to success, but the key to failure is trying to please everybody. — Bill Cosby*

A person who has a good attitude reacts differently to defeat than a person who doesn't. A person with a good attitude will not accept defeat. He will convert it into a steppingstone toward an even greater goal. Sometimes what seems to be defeat can be turned into a blessing in disguise. It can help you keep going toward an even better victory.

The victories recorded in history also talk about the struggle to reach that victory. A wrong attitude will throw you off-course. Outward situations have very little to do with our habits. If you are going to have victory, it has to come from inside, from your attitude.

No great leader was ever a negative, pessimistic individual. Put some fizz in your life by being optimistic. When you shake a bottle of soda, you have fizz that explodes over everything when you remove your thumb. Your enthusiasm can flow over the top, too.

Helen Keller and Napoleon are great illustrations. Napoleon had everything that men usually want. He had power, he had riches and glory. But he said he had never known six happy days in his life. Helen Keller, who was both blind and deaf, declared, "I have found life so beautiful."

If you allow people or circumstances to mess up your attitude, you are giving up the control God gave you. Only you can control your attitude, so if it's messed up, you did it yourself. Something may have happened that you didn't like, and you allowed it to affect you negatively. Just remember that God gives you control over your own mind and attitude.

Too often, your actions follow your feelings. It's possible, however, to improve your feelings with positive actions. It's impossible to remain depressed when helping someone else. Try it. If you're feeling down, go out of your way to do something nice for someone, buy them a cup of coffee, speak a friendly word, or just give them a smile. You'll be surprised at how much better you feel.

> *No person was ever honored for what he received, only for what he accomplished or gave. — Calvin Coolidge*

We live in a great age with progress all around us. Some people believe that these are only hard times with no opportunities to succeed. Success is not a set of circumstances, it is a set of attitudes and decisions — a journey, not the destination.

You may not succeed the first time around, but with a positive attitude, perseverance, and God's help, you will succeed.

Reaching a goal can be fun, even if it takes several attempts. If your attitude concentrates on the positive aspects of the journey, you are more likely to reach the goal. A person who has a positive attitude can inspire the same outlook in others.

You have the power to choose the attitude you want, why not have a good one? When we talk about attitude, it's important to remember that God has given you total, complete control over your mind, which affects your attitude. Throw out the negatives. He gives you the right of control, to think your own thoughts, to control your own attitude.

> *Secret number five: Keep a good attitude in every circumstance.*

Secret 6

FAITH — Your Decisions

Faith will help you make correct decisions. Jesus said, "But seek ye first the kingdom of God, and his righteousness; and all these things shall be added unto you." (Matt. 6:33). I believe putting God first is the bottom line, and should be the first major decision you make. Faith will help you make that decision.

You can't just sit by and expect God to do it all. You decide to move on to success or to fall backwards to failure. It's your decision.

Our church wanted to do something about the "bus kids" who came on Sunday morning without breakfast. Some were sitting in class nearly comatose, others were cross and disruptive. The children's pastor sent notes to the kitchen committee, asking for some meal plans and suggestions.

Some suggested a sweet roll or piece of fruit on the bus on the way to church, others had other "quick and easy" ideas. One person (my daughter, Becki) felt differently. She said, "Many of these children have little or nothing done just for them at home. Most of their nutrition comes from the meals they get at school. Let's fix a real breakfast, so that they will remember that this church cares."

The first Sunday that the plan was tried, Becki felt a tug on her skirt. She looked down to see two children, ages approximately five and seven. The older of the two said very politely, "Thank you for breakfast, you should do this more often."

Becki explained that the church would be having breakfast every Sunday from then on. His face lit up and he said to his little sister, "Oh, goody! We get to eat on the weekends!"

Now every Sunday morning over 100 hungry children are fed cheese, juice, and fruit. They also get an entree that may be cereal, scrambled eggs, pancakes, or waffles. This happens because someone decided to do more than just the minimum.

Don't always be influenced by the opinions of others or you will never make proper decisions. God gave you a brain and a mind, so use it. Gather all the facts before making an important decision.

> *Every day you make a choice, either you exercise faith and feast in the abundance of God's supply, or you give in to the devil and fear, and suffer personal famine. — John Avanzini*

Success in any chosen endeavor is a two-fold decision. First, have faith that you can do it; second, work to achieve it. The first step toward the solution of any problem is the decision it is solvable and that you are going to solve it.

Life is a challenge. When your mind is full of negatives, clutter, jealousy, and unforgiveness, you can't make good decisions. Some people can see opportunities, but don't take them. All our decisions should be based on positive values.

> *Again and again, the impossible problem is solved when we see that the problem is only a tough decision waiting to be made.*
> — *Robert Schuller*

Making a decision is important. The vice president of a large manufacturing company had developed a new product. Research indicated that it would probably meet buyer resistance, but thousands of dollars had already gone in to its development, production, and promotion.

The company attempted to market it through its normal sales force. The salesmen found that they could not sell the product. They met with comments like "too seasonal," "the public isn't ready for that," "it's too big a gamble to stock."

Finally, one salesman was offered a good salary and a permanent position with the company if he would SELL the product. They didn't hear from him for two weeks. Then he appeared with a large bundle of orders.

He needed the job, so he decided to sell the product. He went to dealers, offices, people on the street, and even door to door, creating a market and convincing people that they needed what he had. He was so successful that he soon had to build and train a sales force to handle the volume of demand.

He became vice president of the company. His education was limited; he had no background in sales. The difference was that he needed the job, and decided that he would believe in and sell the product. His decision overcame the negatives.

You might think that you don't have a talent because you've never done something. How do you know that you can't, if you haven't tried? We often discover abilities that we didn't know existed when we try new things. Many skills can be developed by practice.

> *Achieving anything you want is knowing what you want and paying the price for it.*
> — *Jim Agard*

During World War II, the United States needed ships, and needed them quickly. Henry Kaiser was sure that he could build them, even though he had never built even one ship. His friends called him a fool for bidding on the contracts. He not only got the contracts, he built the ships. He didn't know that he couldn't do it, so he did it.

Few of us will ever have to build ships for

the United States government. Most of us won't ever paint a masterpiece, design a $5,000 gown, or compose a symphony. We can, however, learn to draw stick figures for the delight of our grandchildren and play "Chopsticks" on the piano, if we decide not just to try, but to do something. You can make things happen. You can touch others, build a business, bless the church, and win others to Christ, all through faith in God.

Defeat doesn't make you a failure; accepting defeat and refusing to try again does. Some people are so busy failing, they don't have time to succeed. People who have a low sense of self-esteem usually do not accomplish much. God loves you and placed a high value on you. It's not wrong to love what He loves.

> *The depth of our love is in direct proportion to the value we place upon a person or object.*
> *— Kenneth Broadus*

In working to live healthy, prosperous, dedicated Christian lives, we must decide that because God is true, and He has promised to go with us, nothing else can hinder us. Real success is more than just a destination, it is a journey. It's a decision.

You will not just float into the harbor of success. You must decide on the harbor you are seeking. You will not reach any destination that you are not sailing toward.

Nothing in life just happens by accident. Someone makes it happen. It doesn't just snow or rain. Conditions in the atmosphere that are controlled by God cause it to happen.

A person who is successful has simply formed a habit of doing things that unsuccessful people will not do. Some decisions are already made for us, and are not easily altered; our ethnic background, our adult height, the color of our eyes, the color of our hair. (The last two can be changed, at least temporarily.)

> *If at first you don't succeed, break the mold. — Rich Wilkerson*

My mother was bustling around trying to get us fed and off to school. "What do you want for breakfast?" she asked.

"Anything," was my answer.

"Grapefruit and toast or bananas and cereal?"

"Are the bananas the way I like them?"

"Yes."

"Okay, that's what I'll take."

There was a pause. Then Mom asked, "Why don't you want grapefruit and toast?"

I said, "Why can't I have bananas and cereal?"

She replied, "I gave them to your sisters."

She had already decided what I would have. Why did she bother to ask me to make a decision?

Sometimes we make decisions based on other people. This may be good or it may be bad.

People may influence you in a negative way and thereby cause your decision to be flawed. Remember, a successful leader is a person who makes the right move at the right moment and with the right motive.

Don't spend a dollar's worth of time on a ten-cent decision.

I went to a car lot when I was 17 years old to trade my car. The salesman walked around my car several times, looking it over closely. He pointed out every nick and blemish. His remark was, "You aren't going to trade in this crate, are you?" I answered vehemently,

"No, I'm not!"

I left there and drove to another lot. The salesman looked my jalopy over and remarked, "Well, you've cleaned this up pretty well. We can give you a good trade in."

I found a car that I wanted, test drove it, and bought it. I traded my old car in. He probably didn't give me very much for mine, but he made me feel appreciated. I made my decision based on his positive attitude toward my old car.

> *Failure is the opportunity to begin again, and more intelligently.*
> *— Henry Ford*

If you don't have something specific in mind, you are really in trouble. You have to realize that the first step to achieve success is to decide specifically what it is you want, and when you want to achieve it. You can't build anything on what you intend to do. A lot of people intend a lot of things, and accomplish very little. Others may throw their goals overboard at the first sign of opposition. Decide to persist, no matter what happens. Temporary defeat can be a steppingstone to victory. You cannot escape the responsibility of tomorrow by evading it today.

Get your tide up, and your boat will float.

An optimistic person always surrounds himself with others who share his spirit of optimism, even if he is more successful than they are. Being successful attracts more success. Optimists have a peace that others don't understand. They have a belief that they can make things turn out right. They feel that their decisions were right and proper, and they are not afraid of the future. They have a powerful advantage.

> *Success is a decision.*
> *— Dexter Yager*

Decisions are risky because they require you to take a stand for your beliefs. When you know your values and principles, it's easier to make decisions. When you make correct decisions, your future will be blessed. Decide now that things will change for the better in your life. When you have a purpose, you can make the word "impossible" of no importance to you.

Decide:

A. Your dreams are possible.

B. Your plans will be formulated and you have the willpower to carry them through.

C. Your goals will be reached. Write them down.

Anyone who really plans to succeed at anything must be willing to burn the bridges and cut off every avenue of defeat.

We should all do that when we marry, and decide that this is our mate, no matter what. A decision to marry should be based on love and friendship, not on how things appear.

A man telephoned his wife and said, "I'd like to bring our daughter's boyfriend to dinner tonight."

"Oh, no," the wife answered, "not tonight. The cupboard is bare, I've got a cold, my hair is a mess, the furnace is broken, the kids are sick, and the house is a mess."

"I know," said the man. "That's why I want to bring him home tonight. They're planning on getting married."

> *Secret number six: Make right decisions, based upon positive input.*

Secret 7

FAITH — Kills Excuses

Excuses, we've all heard them. Here are 45 that are commonly used. Read them and see how foolish most of them really are.

1. We tried that before.

2. Our situation is different.

3. It's beyond my responsibility.

4. It costs too much.

5. It's not my job.

6. I'm too busy.

7. It's too radical.

8. I don't have the time.

9. I don't have enough help.

10. Let's do research first.

11. It's not practical.

12. My staff will never buy it.

13. Bring it up in a year.

14. It's against policy.

15. We don't have the authority.

16. Let's get back to reality.

17. Why change?

18. It's not our problem.

19. I don't like the idea.

20. You might be right, but. . . .

21. You're years ahead of your time.

22. No one is ready for that.

23. Everyone in our area saw it before.

24. It isn't in the budget.

25. Can't teach an old dog new tricks.

26. Good thought, but impractical.

27. Let's think about it.

28. The administration would never go for it.

29. Let's put it in writing.

30. Where did you dig that one up?

31. We are doing all right without it.

32. It's never been tried before.

33. Let's form a committee.

34. Parents won't like it.

35. I don't see the connection.

36. It won't work in our system.

37. What you are really saying is. . . .

38. Maybe that will work in your area, but not in mine.

39. Don't you think we should look into it further before we act?

40. Let's all sleep on it.

41. It can't be done.

42. It's too much trouble.

43. I know someone who tried it and failed.

44. It's impossible.

45. We've always done it this way.

Don't let negative excuses destroy your will, your ambition, your desires, your dreams.

> *In times like these, it helps to recall that there have always been times like these. — Paul Harvey*

Quentin Edwards has preached to millions in his more than 25 visits to India. Newspaper accounts reported crowds reached 1.2 million. He says that 99 percent of faith is simply obedience.

> *Sorrow — looks back. Worry —*
> *looks around. Faith — looks up.*
> *— Quentin Edwards*

Weak desires breed excuses. If your wood won't burn, it's wet with excuses. When excuses plague your mind, you're defeated before you start. Don't let excuses hold you back.

Excuses and procrastination are twins. Procrastination is usually linked to negativity. Procrastination and positive patience are not the same. Delaying an important decision until you have the facts can be an intelligent move. When you have the facts, decide. Don't leave things in limbo.

Patience is the willingness to wait long enough for a process to produce results. It shouldn't be confused with passive acceptance. Knowledge is important. You get the facts about a situation, understand it, and develop a timing of when to do what.

While I was writing this chapter, I was at O'Hare Airport in Chicago. I was flying on a free ticket, which has a lot of restrictions. The flight to my destination was delayed, and finally canceled. The agent informed me that they had no other flight to my destination until the next day. I smiled and said, "That's all right, you can put me on another airline."

"Not on a free ticket," was her response.

I continued smiling, but refused to accept her decision. I asked her to keep checking. She finally did put me on another airline. As I thanked her, she said, "Why wouldn't you accept my legitimate excuses?"

"I have to be there today," I replied.

"What if it wouldn't have worked?" she asked.

I answered, "IT DID, DIDN'T IT?"

> Secret number seven: Kill all the excuses in your life.

Secret 8

FAITH — Its Process

Let's talk about the process of faith. The Bible gives us a good example of this process in Mark 5:25-34. Let's start by telling the story, using the New King James Version:

> Now a certain woman had a flow of blood for twelve years, and had suffered many things from many physicians. She had spend all that she had and was no better, but rather grew worse.
>
> When she heard about Jesus, she came behind Him in the crowd and touched His garment. For she said "If only I may touch his clothes, I shall be made well." Immediately the

fountain of her blood was dried up, and she felt in her body that she was healed of her affliction.

And Jesus, immediately knowing in Himself that power had gone out of Him, turned around in the crowd and said, "Who touched my clothes?"

But His disciples said to Him, "You see the multitude thronging You, and You say, 'Who touched me?'" And He looked around to see her who had done this thing.

But the woman, fearing and trembling, knowing what had happened to her, came and fell down before Him and told Him the whole truth. And He said to her, "Daughter, your faith has made you well. Go in peace, and be healed of your affliction."

There were six steps which the woman went through.

#1. The woman **knew she was sick**. She had been sick for 12 years. She had lived every day with a condition which made her a social outcast. There was no denying that the problem was there. She had spent everything she had, but instead of getting well, she got progressively worse.

There is a teaching that if you have a headache, measles, chicken pox, or whatever, just say that you don't have it. Paul wrote, "Who calleth those things which be not as though they were" (Rom. 4:17). *It did not say* to call those things which are as though they were not.

We cannot deny sickness: If my nose is running and I'm coughing, I have a cold; if my joints ache, I may have arthritis. We can call forth healing. Say, "I'm fighting (whatever);" not "I'm so sick." Say, "God is healing me, 'by His stripes we are healed.' " Notice that there is a difference in attitude. Neither one denies the problem, but one claims an answer while the other only emanates despair. There must always be a balance.

#2. She **knew that Jesus could and would heal her**. She had heard of the miracles which He had done for others. She had heard that blind eyes were opened, cripples walked, and the dead were raised. She raised her level of belief. Everyone knows He can, but this woman knew He would. There was no doubt in her mind whatsoever.

> *The depth of your relationship with God will determine your level of faith.* — Sam Smucker

Sometimes faith is born in desperation. Sometimes it comes because hearing something over and over spurs our faith to work. Sometimes it is like a small seed planted in good ground. It is watered and fertilized and grows until that one seed is duplicated hundreds of times over.

You know that Jesus can meet your need, but do you know He will? Let the process of faith begin for your needs.

#3. She **established a "faith image."** She envisioned herself being healed. Dave Williams says, "Enjoy a faith movie." She remembered how strong and healthy she had felt before this thing started. The eyes of faith see differently than our natural eyes.

Sometimes it seems that it's easier for God to do a difficult thing than an easy one, because with the easy thing, we mix in human reasoning and conclude that it probably would have happened anyway. With a hard thing, we just give up and say, "God, it's in Your hands." When we get out of the way, He can take over and create our miracle.

She understood that faith isn't something you get, it's something you already have. We need to train our faith in the proper channels, to start the process of faith.

> *If God always gave us everything*
> *we wanted on a silver platter, we'd*
> *never have any faith.*
> *— "Woody" Clark*

#4. The woman **established a time and a place for her deliverance**. There is a pattern with decisions. We don't say that sometime, some doctor in some hospital will operate on me. When we want medical help, we say "On such and such a day at a certain time, I'm going to have to have Dr.

What's—His—Name remove the wart from my little toe" (or whatever).

You can't steer a parked car. You have to put it into gear and begin to move before anything happens.

#5. She **overcame the obstacles**. She was sick, she was weak, she was suffering, she was poor, she was a woman in a culture which put little value on women. Her faith was tested. Everything was against her, but she had envisioned the end result, so obstacles became steppingstones to the answer.

#6. And finally, she **closed her case in victory**. She believed, she obeyed, and refused to give up and she had victory. She climbed over every mountain of unbelief and impossibility and reached an altitude of answered prayer. The devil is against you and God is for you. Whichever side you choose wins.

Secret number eight: Get into the process of faith and follow through to the result.

Secret 9

FAITH — Your Sins

Faith puts God's energy to work for you. "Whatsoever is not of faith is sin" (Rom. 14:23). So when you are thinking in a negative manner that God is not going to do what He promised, it is sin. Sin is separation from God.

> *When we come to the end of ourselves, we come to the beginning of God. He will forgive and help us.*
> *— Monty Hipp*

"Ye ask, and receive not, because ye ask amiss, that ye may consume it upon your lusts" (James 4:3).

Worry will drive us to hurry so that we don't miss out. God doesn't always operate in haste. He gives us time to do what is necessary for us. He can take care of His part quickly when His time comes.

Matthew, Mark, and Luke all relate the story of Jairus, one of the rulers of the synagogue in Capernaum. Jesus was teaching by the sea when Jairus came to Him. He begged Him to come to his house and heal his daughter, who was dying.

Jesus went with him. On the way, the healing which we talked about in chapter eight took place. Can't you imagine how much Jairus must have resented this interruption? Then the unthinkable happened; his servants came to tell them that the girl was dead.

Jesus responded by telling Jairus to quit being afraid and keep on believing, even after his daughter had died. Sometimes things seem to go from bad to worse, but when God starts a journey with you, He'll finish it with you, if you keep believing.

God's sovereignty will do a lot of things, but God wants us to trust Him. God's sovereignty will not cause us to live a holy life. We have a choice. We have to believe and act on that belief. Don't doubt, say to yourself that God will work a miracle, then trust Him.

Poor Jairus. When they reached the house, the mourners were already there. Everyone laughed at the idea that the child was only sleeping. It's sometimes hard to hang on to our faith when our friends ridicule us, so Jesus put them all outside except the girl's parents and Peter, James, and John.

The apostle Peter wrote, "Humble yourselves therefore under the mighty hand of God, that He may exalt you in due time: Casting all your care upon Him; for he careth for you. Be sober, be vigilant; because your adversary the devil, as a roaring lion, walketh about, seeking whom he may devour" (1 Pet. 5:6-8).

A lion doesn't roar when he's hunting. He roars after he has made the capture to scare off others who may want his kill. Peter is saying to deal with anxiety now, because it becomes sin when we worry. If we continue in it, Satan will come and devour us because we won't stop sin when it starts.

Even when we sin, our sins don't have to devour us. They only devour us when we continue in them, and they are manifested in a mature way. Sin has to come to a place of accomplishment before it brings forth death.

Lust that is not dealt with swiftly can lead to adultery and a broken marriage. Or it can be dealt with early, asking God's forgiveness, and have no negative results.

Anger that is not dealt with can lead to bitterness. Bitterness causes unforgiveness, which makes you critical. It begins to devour you and destroy everything around you. If we deal with the sin of anger when it first hits our spirit, and repent of it, it has no chance to devour us.

God's mercy and love forgives our sin, when we ask Him (1 John 1:9). When we walk with Him and desire His best in our lives, He helps us through our tests and strengthens our faith.

Jairus faith had been put to the ultimate test.

Not very much is told about his reaction to the interruption caused by the healing of the woman or the news of his daughter's death. But put yourself in his place. He must have been frustrated. He may have been discouraged. His emotions probably felt like a yo-yo.

Then Jesus took the girl by the hand and said, "Child, get up."

All the doubt and fear and discouragement had to vanish instantly. His daughter got up and walked, and like any healthy, normal child, she needed to eat. Jesus' love and compassion had triumphed over all the obstacles.

In our own lives, circumstances can cause us to doubt and worry and lose faith. God controls the circumstances, and His timing is flawless.

> *Secret number nine: Don't allow*
> *sin to hinder your faith.*

Secret 10

FAITH — Versus Fear

We often are afraid of the things we don't know or understand. Some may fear success or maybe failure. Some are afraid to leave their comfort zone.

> God hath not given us the spirit of fear; but of power, and of love, and of a sound mind (2 Tim. 1:7).

> *You never conquer a mountain, because mountains cannot be conquered; you conquer yourself: your hopes, your fears. — Jim Whittaker, first American to reach the summit of Mt. Everest*

Matthew tells of a time when Peter walks on the water to Jesus during a storm on the Sea of Galilee.

The disciples had started across the sea, leaving Jesus behind. A storm had arisen on the lake. The boat was battered by waves and heavy winds and the disciples were frightened. When they saw Jesus walking on the water, they became more frightened, thinking it was a ghost.

When the Lord speaks, courage arises. "Faith comes by hearing . . . the Word of God." Peter's response was classic, "Lord, IF it is You, bid me come to You."

Peter undoubtedly knew that this was Jesus. He said, "Bid me come to You on the water." Why would he want that? The sea was rough, and the wind was blowing. He knew that when He was in the presence of Jesus, no fear could touch him. He wanted to get closer to the Lord. He figured that it was preferable to be next to Jesus than to be in the boat fighting the storm.

Jesus said, "Come on, Peter." Peter got out of the boat and walked on the water toward Jesus. This wasn't nice, calm, glassy smooth water. It was an extremely rough lake storm, but Peter walked on the water.

> *Peter is the only man who ever really went overboard in his faith.*
> *— Herschel Gammill*

Why do you suppose God allowed Peter to

walk on the water? Maybe because God wanted things to happen that would draw Peter closer to Jesus. He was doing fine until he looked around. Peter's fear came when he began to look at the circumstances. We need to realize what our circumstances are, but not to look at them in such a way that they overwhelm us. They can bring fear into our life.

Peter cried, "Lord, save me." Jesus asked him (after they were in the boat), "Why did you doubt?" In other words, "You started out pretty well, why did you let the circumstances get to you? Don't look at the circumstances and the hurdles and the storms. Look with faith at the things that aren't seen, because they are the things which will bring real victory into your life."

Blessings won't attack you, you must be prepared to receive them. People who succeed in anything in life have to recognize the causes of failure. Faith means taking action.

> *Faith is needed for the impossible.*
> *You dare to act on the Word as*
> *though the impossible had become a*
> *possibility, a reality.*
> *— E.W. Kenyon*

The story is told of two hoboes sitting against a tree by a river. "You know, Bob, this business of trampin' your way through life jest ain't what it's cracked up ta be. Think about et. Sleepin' in parks on col' benches, in the woods 'nd under bridges;

trav'lin' on freight trains; bein' dogged by the p'leece; bein' kicked frum town to town. We ain't wunted, 'nd we're laffed at ever'where we go!" lamented the first one.

"Well, Sam," chided the other, "If thet's how ya feel 'bout et, whyn't cha go 'nd find yerself a job?"

"What?" exclaimed Sam in amazement, "'nd admit I'm a failure?"

> *Ransomed men need no longer pause in fear to enter the Holy of Holies, God wills that we should push on into His presence and live our whole lives there.*
> — *A.W. Tozer*

When His presence is in our life, fear and things like that just fade away. When we feel that He is there, there is no fear. When His presence is not as tangible, then fear tries to come into our mind. Faith is the channel through which God can work. The more we can believe in Him, and in what He can do, the more Christ can manifest himself.

You can have faith without fear, but you cannot have fear without faith. Fear is taking belief, and putting it in the wrong thing, which is what produces the fear. If you have fear, your faith is in the wrong place.

When we find Christ, God gives us a measure of faith. He gives us the ability to trust in Him and His Word, then there should no room for fear in our life.

If we use that ability toward the things of this world, there will be very little faith in our lives. That faith will not remove mountains. That faith will not get our needs met. Get into the habit of exercising faith.

> *Faith is knowing that God will never let you down. — Paul Fisher*

Habits are developed by repeating an action over and over until it becomes a natural reaction. Good habits can be developed to replace bad habits. We can get into the habit of always being late or we can make ourselves allow a few extra minutes and be habitually early. The choice is ours. We make our habits, but in the end, our habits make us.

Does it seem that Jesus always waits until the last minute? Maybe He does that to test our faith. He lets us come to the end of ourselves to test our faith. Then we come to the beginning of God. The disciples had probably spent several hours on the lake, fighting the storm. They had been driven far out into the middle of the lake as the wind blew. Imagine trying to row a boat big enough for 12 to 15 people for that long. Their level of fear was probably very high.

The disciples were afraid. One other account of the story says that Jesus walked as if He was going to pass the boat. Why did Jesus do this? Jesus wants us to want Him. Rather than walk in uninvited and change the situation, He often makes us cry out to Him for help.

Jesus response to their cry of fear was, "Take courage, don't be afraid." Notice the characteristic of faith. Faith is in the offensive position, not the defensive position. It wants to reclaim what fear has taken.

Jesus said, "Take courage."

> *It's time we circled the wagons, pulled out the artillery, and rolled up our sleeves, and readied ourselves to be tough with the devil. — Rod Parsley*

You will never win a war on the shells you fired in the last war. We need new ammunition every day.

A piece of swampland in Louisiana was for sale because the owner had died. Both of the bidders owned land that bordered it. The land was extremely swampy and covered with bamboo. In this condition, it really wasn't suitable for farmland.

One prospective purchaser bid very low; he wouldn't mind increasing his acreage, but he couldn't see that the land was worth very much. The other man's bid was over twice that of his neighbor. He cut the bamboo for fishing poles, which he sold for more than enough to pay for the purchase of the land. What a difference in perspective.

> *Sometimes Christians dig up the*
> *doubts in fear, that they have*
> *planted in faith.*
> *— Jim Agard*

"The nobleman saith unto him, Sir, come down ere my child die" (John 4:49). Jesus said to him, "Go thy way; thy son liveth." The man believed the word that Jesus had said to him, and went his way. As he was going, his servants met him on the way and said that his son was living. He inquired of them when he began to get better, and they said to him, "Yesterday at the seventh hour the fever left him."

There are two familiar types of worry or fear. Some fears can be removed by finding out the facts. Fear of some disease can be squelched by a visit to the doctor. Some fearful realities need the faith of God and His word to give the peace that passes understanding.

When God speaks, it will produce a faith and assurance that will carry us through, even when the situation is terrible. Peter had so much peace in jail that the angel had to wake him up in order to rescue him.

If you feel that God has told you something, and it frightens you, maybe it wasn't God speaking. When the Holy Spirit ministers to a believer, it causes peace, not anxiety. The message is "fear not," or "do not be afraid."

It is said that five basic fears are a fear of poverty, fear of old age or death, fear of loss of love, fear of ill health, and fear of criticism. Before you can conquer an enemy, you must understand it, know how that enemy operates, know its habits, and who it "hangs out" with.

Some psychologists tell us that we are born with only two fears: a fear of loud noises, and a fear of falling. All other fears are the result of the experiences which have come into our lives. These fears would control our lives, if we let them.

Certain types of fear are not a bad thing. Experience has taught us to be afraid of fire. It has also taught us to fear strange dogs, especially if they are growling at us, and not to walk in the middle of the freeway. This kind of "fear" is more of a healthy respect.

When we allow fears to control our lives — fear of the dark, fear of airplanes, fear of the unknown, fear of height, fear of this, and fear of that, we become captive to our fears. Sometimes, recovering from these fears takes a real deliverance, and a lot of faith, plus a lot of "one step at a time."

I have friends who are afraid of flying, but they have determined that their fear will not keep them from going where they want to go. They have learned to control their fear instead of allowing that fear to control them.

We often quote from the Book of Romans: "Tribulation worketh patience," and forget the rest of the passage. "And patience, experience; and experience, hope: and hope maketh not ashamed" (Rom. 5: 3-5).

Walking through fears, one step at a time, can help us conquer our fears. First, sit down with paper and pen and write down the worst possible thing that could happen if what you are afraid of comes to pass. Next, look at how unlikely it really is to happen. Then, think about how good you will feel when you conquer that fear and do the thing you were afraid of successfully.

If you talk fear, it will increase its grip upon you. If you talk failure, it will hold you in bondage. Instead, we need to talk faith, to talk progress, to talk answers, to talk believing. "What I feared has come upon me; what I dreaded has happened to me. I have no peace, no quietness; I have no rest, but only turmoil" (Job 3:25-26;NIV).

The more you possess, the more you fear its loss. Fear can open the door for Satan. Fear produces more fear. You have the power to conquer fear. "There is no fear in love; but perfect love casteth out fear: because fear hath torment" (1 John 4:18).

> *Call the devil a liar, proclaim Christ is truth. — J. Don George*

If you have a specific, chronic fear or anxiety in your life, you need to go to the word of God. Find out what it has to say about that thing, and find faith in that area. "Faith comes by hearing and . . . by the word of God." When you read the Word of God, God will make it alive to you. You can get victory over that fear, because God does not want us to be controlled by fear. "I sought the Lord, and He heard me, and delivered me from all my fears" (Ps. 34:4).

The best teacher is the Holy Spirit. He is what makes our faith alive. He makes our relationships alive. Worry comes when the presence of the Holy Spirit is less tangible in our lives.

Stress is related to anxiety, which is produced by worry. We need to press in to the presence of God in order to overcome our worries and fears. Some adults have fears which they have carried from childhood. Doctors tell us that ulcers, hypertension, heart disease, and other physical problems can be triggered by fear.

The Bible tells us that we don't walk by sight, we walk by faith. We don't look at things we can see, but at things that are eternal.

If you're having an anxiety attack, sit down and worship the Lord. Focus on the spiritual side and away from the circumstances that are causing your anxieties. Get lost in God's presence. Time with God has a greater, longer lasting effect than time spent exercising physically.

> *You can't walk in fear, and sit down in faith.*
> — *Quentin Edwards*

Fear and faith are like a teeter-totter. When faith goes up, fear decreases. When fear increases, faith decreases. Both fear and faith work from belief.

Some have fear of dying, fear of sickness, fear of flying, fear of one thing or another. How many blessings do we miss because of fear? Fear inhibits; faith gives freedom to act. Our avenue of blessing broadens. Fear confines us to a narrow rut; faith opens the door and gets us out of the rut.

We can have the courage to change our circumstances; our job, our relationships. There may be confrontation, but with faith, we can step through the fear and accomplish what's needed. We can get over our fears of each other, work through our problems, and repair relationships.

Even when the circumstances are bad, we can still "walk on the water," and get to Jesus. We can still get the help we need from God, and feel His presence.

"Be careful for nothing; but in every thing by prayer and supplication with thanksgiving, let your requests be made known unto God" (Phil. 4:6).

Concern and worry are different. Concern does the necessary things to protect from harm. That takes energy and effort. Concern is a virtue. Worry goes beyond concern by not doing what is possible, and failing to give the rest to the Lord.

It takes practice to break the habit of worry, and to become a person of faith. We have a greater ability to receive from God when we refuse to worry. If we seek first the kingdom of God and His righteousness, then ALL these necessities of life will be taken care of (Matt. 6:33; my paraphrase).

David said that he'd been young, and he'd been old, but he'd never seen the righteous forsaken. Obviously, you can live in a way that God will always meet the necessities of your life. Let's get into that mode. God will work with us wherever we are, and lead us on. It's a goal to move toward.

A person who lets fear rule his mind not only ruins the opportunities that come his way, he ruins the opportunities of others he comes in contact with. Never let negatives from others influence you. Close yourself to all that causes you fear, anger, or envy. Let your faith be made more powerful than your fear. Fear is the biggest obstacle to success.

Live in faith, not fear. "Ye shall not fear them; for the Lord your God he shall fight for you" (Deut. 3:22). "For ye have not received the spirit of bondage again to fear" (Rom. 8:15). "God hath not given us the spirit of fear" (2 Tim. 1:7).

You have the protection of God (see Ps. 46:1).

You have the keys to the Kingdom (see Luke 12:31-32).

You have the power to take the land (see Deut. 1:21).

> *Secret number ten: Assassinate the fear in your life. Let faith turn into action.*

Secret 11

FAITH — Rejection

Another hindrance to faith can be a fear of being rejected by our peers. We don't want to seem to be strange or out of step, so we hide our faith.

Someone has said that life is a jungle, and we never get out alive. I plan to, don't you?

> See a faith movie of success and not failure. — Dave Williams

Faith is never stimulated or motivated by any form of fear. Galatians 5:6 tells us "faith worketh by love." In other words, love is the motivation for faith. First John says that there is no fear in love, because perfect love casts out all fear, because fear has torment. Perfected love removes all forms of fear, and faith is motivated by love.

Love is not permissive with our children. It takes control of the child and the situation. It sets definite boundaries for behavior. Fear that the child will reject boundaries can lead to allowing the child to do as he/she pleases. This doesn't show love to the child, nor faith in his/her desire to do the right thing. It also destroys any respect of the child for the parent.

Many sexual sins take place because of a fear of being rejected as a person by the other party. Most sins have an element of fear involved in them. People lie because of fear of the reaction of the person to the truth.

Satan controls the world through fear. Christians should be able to walk in faith and love that expels fear.

Fight off the fear of rejection. We have to be motivated by a love that wants to do positive things, even though we have to step through many circles of rejection. It will step through to bring forth a positive result.

> *A winner is one who accepts his failures and mistakes, picks up the pieces, and continues striving to reach his goals. — Dexter Yager*

If love is operating in my life, there will be no fear there. We need more real love in our lives for our faith to be effective. It has to be the kind of love in which there is an absence of fear, and rejects all fear. It can't be affected by peer pressure, by what others say. It can't be affected by what is popular. It can't be affected by what you think may happen to you. It must only be affected by compassion and love for others. We need to live in faith that is motivated by love.

> *Quit trying to get a miracle on your own, and trust God to do as He promised. — Richard Roberts*

Say to those around you, "I'm no longer afraid of you, I will love you, even if you reject me." Relationships will flourish when we cease to be afraid of or threatened by each other.

She wasn't a pretty child, and she had an annoying personality. None of the other children at the orphanage were friendly to her. Even the teachers considered her a problem and a nuisance.

One day one of the other children ran into the office and reported that she was hanging a note in a tree. The headmistress climbed the tree to get the note. She found a single piece of paper with these words scribbled on it, "To whoever finds this, I love you."

The lonely child was just expressing the need of all of our hearts, to be loved.

Men and women are afraid of each other, but they shouldn't be. Wives shouldn't be afraid of their husbands, that they will be yelled at if things aren't done just to his satisfaction.

God created man to be the head of his home,

but this doesn't give the man the license to govern
as a tyrant. Men shouldn't be afraid of their wives.
The couple needs to work together in love.

> *Birdie made me feel successful*
> *when I was nothing. She is my*
> *secret weapon.*
> — *Dexter Yager*

A successful marriage doesn't happen just
because two people "fall in love." It's the result of
sacrifice and understanding, patience and humility.
It is a masterpiece created by two people who really work at it.

Age-old conflicts and differences exist between men and women. Pretending that they aren't
real often adds to the distrust and frustration.

A man thinks about sexual relations differently than a woman. He is more concerned about
the physical act, while she is more concerned about
the emotional aspect. She wants him to commit to
"be there" and help; he resents being "tied down."

A man wants to feel trusted, while a woman
needs to be cared for. Men want to feel accepted;
women want to be understood. Men want to feel
appreciated, women want to be respected.

When we understand our differences, our relationships improve. A marriage partner is a great
asset and stimulant to a mate's ego when they are
in unity.

Many pastor friends of mine with large
churches, like Randall Ross from Lubbock, Texas,

John Lloyd of Clearwater, Florida, and several others, trust me completely. They ask me to take their pulpit when they are on vacation or out of the country. They know that I would not take unfair advantage of their absence and cause harm to their church. I will only do them good. Therefore our friendships flourish in love.

In Matthew 24, Jesus said that most people's love will wax cold. In Luke 18, speaking about His return, He asks, "When I return, will I find faith on the earth?" Why was He worried about finding faith? Because, before He returns, the love of many will wax cold. Without love, you cannot have the motivation of faith.

Faith is useless without the person of the Holy Spirit. God wants us to have a personal relationship with Him. When we talk about the principles of faith and how to keep fear out of our lives, it is based on that intimate relationship with the Holy Spirit in our lives.

When we realize that we are accepted by God, it can remove the fear of being rejected by others. Paul says that we are made to "sit together in heavenly places" (Eph. 2: 6). What greater acceptance do we need?

> *Secret number eleven: Get the fear of rejection out of your life through love.*

Secret 12

FAITH —
Forgiveness

"Then came Peter to him, and said, Lord, how oft shall my brother sin against me, and I forgive him? til seven times? Jesus saith unto thee, Until seven times: but, Until seventy times seven" (Matt. 18:21-22). If you forgive but don't forget, you allow the problem to grow and fester. That's not really forgiveness.

In today's world, people are encouraged not to forgive, but to sue and take legal action. Some non-Christian counselors say we need to commit an act of anger, an act of revenge to help us gain control. Some enjoy the anger and hatred and desire to get even. It seems crazy and even impossible. Forgiveness is God's way; getting even is Satan's method. If you don't forgive, the pain experienced will stay alive and you will never accomplish anything really productive.

Jesus told us that unless we forgive, God will not forgive us. Even if you are the "victim," forgiveness benefits you. When you hold on to your pain, hurt, hatred, anger, and revenge, it will take its toll on your emotions and even your health. You might feel that the person doesn't deserve forgiveness and refuse. You are right, unless you want the Lord to forgive and bless you.

> *Be quick to repent and quick to forgive and you'll never be far from God. — Kenneth E. Hagin*

Sometimes we even have to love the unlovable. They often need not only our love, but our understanding. We can't hate the person, even when we abhor his actions.

I heard of this incident which happened in one of our major U.S. cities. As a Korean student walked from his apartment to mail a letter, he was attacked and beaten by a group of teenage boys. He died before he could be taken to the hospital.

The boys were promptly identified and arrested. The news media and the community at large demanded the severest action possible.

But the family of the boy, who had been greatly impacted by the ministry of Dr. David Yonggi Cho, felt differently. They wrote the court, asking the greatest degree of leniency be shown to the boys. They even started a fund to help the boys when they were released from prison. Even though they hated the killing of their son, they forgave those who had done it.

When you take revenge, you are stuck to the person who has wronged you, even if that person is no longer part of your life. Forgiving them doesn't mean they were right, it just means you are.

I've seen people who couldn't get a miracle until they asked someone for forgiveness. Maybe you said things which you shouldn't have. You might have to pay someone you cheated. Sometimes you have to get the records straight.

We all like to quote the words of Jesus, "What things soever ye desire, when ye pray, believe that ye receive them, and ye shall have them" (Mark 11:24). We do not so easily quote the passage that follows: "And when ye stand praying, forgive, if ye have ought against any: that your Father also which is in heaven may forgive you your trespasses. But if ye do not forgive, neither will your Father which is in heaven forgive your trespasses" (Matt. 11:25-26). Jesus even mentioned a grudge.

> *Grace has been described as when God treats us like we don't deserve; mercy is when God doesn't treat us like we do deserve. — Jim Menke*

Forgiveness is a canceled note, torn in pieces and thrown into the fire. Unforgiveness can turn into bitterness and destroy you. When you forgive your enemies, it annoys them. Sometimes, because you forgive, your adversary makes things right.

During Jesus' day, the Roman army occupied Palestine. It was a law that if a Jew was asked by a Roman soldier to carry his pack, he had to obey for one mile. The Jews felt victimized by the law.

Jesus said, "Don't just go one mile, go two" (Matt. 5:41). In other words, the Roman soldier has you under his control for the first mile. When you go the second mile, you are free and in control of the situation.

There's really a balance to the whole thing. Having faith is wonderful. Faith and forgiveness will oil the hinges of your doors. If you want God to open the doors and the windows of heaven, faith and forgiveness will get the job done.

> I will bless the Lord at all times: his praise (not unforgiveness and bitterness) shall continually be in my mouth (Ps. 34:1).

In order to have real victories in your life and stay on top of situations, you have to relate to others in a proper manner. Forgiveness is part of relating.

> *Faith is recalling that I grow, not by trying, but by trusting.*
> — *W.H. Heaston*

When we allow what someone has done against us to bother us, we are giving the offender power over us; power over our blood pressure, power over our sleep, power over our health. They may be dancing with joy knowing that we are worrying about them. You don't need this turmoil in your life.

We must learn to forgive and flush these things from our life. It doesn't matter whether it's something that has been said or an unpaid debt. Maybe the offender has somehow justified it to himself. It shouldn't matter to us.

One of the chief personality characteristics of people with hypertension or high blood pressure is resentment. When resentment is chronic, chronic hypertension and heart trouble often follow. Jesus was telling us how to keep from having high blood pressure, heart trouble, ulcers, and other ailments.

Forgive 70 times 7. If you harbor hatred, your food will not digest properly. Your nights will be restless. It can hinder your ability to work, and definitely your success. It costs you. It takes strength to forgive. The weak don't do it.

You may feel that you can't love your enemies. At least love yourself enough in order to not permit your enemies to control your life and future.

> *When the storms of life strike, it's what happens IN you that determines what will happen TO you. — Jerry Savelle*

Proverbs says that a soft answer turns away wrath. You can actually determine no one will disturb you or make you angry. As children we learned, "Sticks and stones may break my bones, but names will never hurt me." One sure way to forgive those who have wronged you, and become bigger than yourself in doing so, is to refuse to let things get to you. They don't make you "mad," you allow yourself to get "mad" because of the situation. Your attitude is very important. Keep a good attitude of forgiveness.

In 1918, it was rumored that the German propagandists were arousing the blacks and inciting them to rebellion. Lawrence Jones was a black preacher and teacher in Mississippi. One night in a sermon he stated, "Let's rise up and fight."

Whites outside who were looking for a reason to attack, rushed into the church, grabbed him and dragged him for nearly a mile, intending to hang him from a tree. They piled up wood for him to stand on, so that he could be hanged and burned at the same time. One man yelled, "Let him speak before he dies!"

He said, "I don't hate those who dragged me up the road to hang and burn me. I've been too busy with my ministry, helping people. I'm too absorbed in something bigger than myself. I have no time to quarrel, no time for regrets, and no man can force me to stoop low enough to hate."

As he spoke with sincere and moving eloquence, he pleaded for this cause, and the mob began to soften. Then an old Confederate soldier stood up and said, "I believe he's right, and we're wrong.

Let's do something to help him."

The mob was moved by his sincerity and attitude of forgiveness. Not only did they release him, they took an offering to help him in his cause.

The prayer of the Sioux Indian is: "O Great Spirit, keep me from ever judging or criticizing a man until I have walked in his moccasins for two weeks."

You can't be a brighter star by blowing out everyone else's candle. You'll just live in a darker world. Keep your mind on the Word of God and let it become a part of your life.

When we try to get even with our enemies, we hurt ourselves more than we ever hurt them. That's why forgiveness is important.

Someone who was very close to me cost me a lot of money. I co-signed a note for him, with his promise to pay as agreed. He defaulted after only a few payments, and I had to repay the note. It was hard for me to forgive him, but when I did, God blessed me in financial ways.

Maybe you're wondering what this has to do with faith. When you forgive and have a right spirit, God will bless you. My close friend, Dan Wold, said that someone who owed him money went broke. But Dan kept a good spirit and prospered, even without the money owed to him.

> *If we exchange forgiveness for bad treatment, we win. — Dan Wold*

A father and son were disagreeing. The son

decided to leave and move to another state. The father gave him a letter as he left and said, "Son, take this letter, and when you get to where you are going, open it and read it. Don't open it before then."

The son finally settled in a distant state, and opened the letter. He read, "You're hundreds of miles from home, and yet you don't feel any different, do you? I knew you wouldn't, because you have taken with you the one thing that's the cause of all the troubles that you have, that is yourself. It isn't the situation that we disagreed on, it's yourself. As a man thinketh in his heart, so is he. When you realize that, son, come home, for you will be cured of your problem."

The letter angered the son greatly. He went for a walk to calm down. As he walked, he passed a church. The minister was preaching on the text, "He who conquers his spirit is mightier than he who takes a city." He realized that his father had spoken the truth. He was shocked to really see himself as he was, disagreeing with his father. He packed up and traveled back home, having conquered his spirit.

I'm convinced that our peace of mind and our joy in living don't depend on where we are or what we have or who we are, but on our attitude. God wants to be our source, our daily sustenance.

A person who doesn't forgive will never have peace of mind, or accomplish success. Unforgiveness is a destructive emotion that blocks your way to success. It unplugs your "blessing machine."

Reportedly, IBM's Tom Watson was asked if he was going to fire an employee whose mistake had cost IBM $600,000. He said, "No, I just spent $600,000. training him, why would I want someone to hire his experience?"

> *Secret number twelve: Forgive all wrongs against you and you will prosper.*

Secret 13

FAITH — Building Crew

Faith is wonderful, isn't it? In the church world, there's the building crew and the wrecking crew. On the building crew, you give, serve, tell, share, bless, help, sacrifice, go, do for others what you'd like somebody to do for you, and so on. Faith puts you on the building crew.

All the great leaders that I know are on the building crew. They create encouragement and excitement, they are dream builders. They look at the positive side, they are prophets of sunshine.

> *The ultimate leader is one who is willing to develop people to the point that they eventually surpass him (or her) in knowledge and ability. — Fred A. Manske, Jr.*

On the wrecking crew, you tear down, you grumble, gripe, and criticize — and nothing is ever right.

Too many people live on the negative side. They are a negative force. They breed discouragement and confusion, tearing down dreams and destroying goals. These prophets of gloom are dedicated agitators.

> *A leader takes people where they want to go. A great leader takes people where they don't necessarily want to go, but ought to be.*
> — *Rosalynn Carter*

Here in Yakima there are lots of orchards. My uncle and aunt, John and Hellen Barnes, usually see that we are well-supplied with apples, which I love. I got into the habit of grabbing an apple from a box in the garage on my way to the office every morning.

One day I saw a bad apple in the box, but didn't deal with it. Instead, I took my apple from the other side of the box. Within a few days, I discovered that every apple that touched the bad apple had also turned bad.

That should be a lesson to us. Don't hang out with bad apples, with people who are skeptical and negative. I would rather be called gullible than refuse to believe anything. Choose people with faith as your closest friends.

A man who leads the orchestra must turn

his back to the crowd.

You say Christians don't have problems. I speak in prisons, and I don't tell them that if they give their lives to God, they'll get out tomorrow. I tell them that you can be free and live in a cell. There are people walking the streets who aren't free.

I talk often to a young man who is in prison for something he didn't do. I tell him "Have faith, God is big, and you can be free and live in a cell. Have a ministry there. You know God, help others find Him. It's going to get better. God has you there for a reason, even though it's hard to understand."

Faith and attitude work together. Faith will put you on the building crew. When you find people who are constantly finding fault with everything, they're on the wrecking crew. They need to get on the building crew. The men mentioned in the eleventh chapter of Hebrews were all on the building crew, real leaders.

> *It isn't the people you fire who make your life miserable, it's the people you don't.*
> *— Harvey Mackay*

When you are on the building crew, your mind will be alert, looking for creative ways to bless others. You will desire to associate with others who are also positive and on the building crew.

When the people around you are constantly negative, it will tear you down. You may find that

you want to reassess who it is that you spend a lot
of time with. It takes courage to be a builder-upper.
You can make the changes that it takes to be a leader.
Most "winners" were once classed as "losers."

> *Secret number thirteen: Get on the*
> *building crew.*

Secret 14

FAITH — Without Compromise

What we need is uncompromising faith that holds strong against criticism, persecution, and all of Satan's other devices. You may change methods, but never compromise your principles. The dictionary defines principles as a basic truth, a rule or concept. It also says that a method is a system, a way, or process.

From birth, we have been trained to take the easiest route. We ride instead of walk. There is an adage that "Necessity is the mother of invention." There is a corollary for that: "Laziness is the mother of efficiency." That's okay for most things.

When our Christian values are challenged, we should never, under any circumstances, lower our standards. God wants us to keep our values high, no matter the cost. High standards may cost you, but the rewards are worth it.

Some college "jocks" were teasing the only one among them who was about to graduate and was still a virgin. His answer was, "If at any time I want to be like you, I can. However, never in your lives can you be like me, no matter how badly you want to."

> *Faith clamps down the teeth of God's Word on the seat of the enemy's pants and hangs on until Satan quits.* — *Marilyn Hickey*

Satan will try to keep us from the good things of God. But there is power if we persevere. The spirit of God falls on those who have strong convictions. We won't be much of a light in the darkened world if we don't have strong convictions.

> See to it that no one takes you captive through hollow and deceptive philosophy, which depends on human tradition and the basic principles of this world rather than on Christ. (Col. 2:8;NIV).

Evidently, someone was causing problems within the church at Colosse and causing the Christians to leave the path of righteousness and go into sin. Philosophy is a man-made perspective of truth.

Pragmatism is one philosophy which says "Do whatever it takes to reach the goal." Ethics don't matter. It doesn't matter if it costs you respect. The end justifies the means. Just get the job done. Take the easy route.

This is the wrong perspective.

Marriage to an unbeliever is strongly forbidden by the Bible. But it's easy to rationalize, maybe he/she is the only chance I'll have. He/she claims to believe, maybe after we're married he/she will change. Many lives have been ruined with this thought. The dating game is a poor mission field.

If you have to throw out your quality in order to achieve quantity, forget it. Quantity without quality is worthless. Take quality and do things God's way. He'll give you a quantity that's full of quality.

Don't let worldly pragmatism influence your methods of ministry, in prospering at home, or in climbing the ladder of success. Don't let down your ethics. Don't lose your values.

Don't compromise your faith. The results are not pleasing to God. Some natural knowledge may help you achieve the goal, but if it goes against ethics and values, it may cost you your integrity. It's not worth it.

Compromise usually begins small, but can grow so strong that it eventually destroys your faith. Stop the compromise while there is still a chance to be saved.

Be uncompromising, strong, dogmatic, full of conviction, and God will bless you. When you first begin to do this, you may feel weak, but the longer you practice it, the bolder you become.

Do keep an open mind where new methods

are concerned. Altering some methods without compromising our principles might help us touch more lives. The apostle Paul said it very well, "I am made all things to all men, that I might by all means save some" (1 Cor. 9:22).

The Book of Daniel tells the story of four young men who refused to compromise. Although they were captives in a strange land, they held fast to the convictions they had been taught. Daniel was just a youth, but he had strong faith that put older men to shame.

This was the first time Jerusalem was besieged. Isaiah had warned them that if they didn't obey God, God would judge them and put them into captivity. They didn't listen, so judgment fell. They were taken captive, their sons were taken to Babylon, and they were scattered. The land got its rest.

There was a belief that if you had the vessels of a certain deity, you had authority over that deity. Nebuchadnezzar took some of the vessels from the temple back to Babylon to show the people that their god was more powerful than Jehovah, not realizing that Jehovah had purposely decided to judge Israel. That was the only reason that they had victory over Jerusalem.

In order to ensure the cooperation of the king of Judah, Nebuchadnezzar literally took hostages, 50 to 75 teenage boys.

Daniel was a youth who would not compromise his faith. He was separated from his family and taken to a strange land to become trained to be an official in the court of a heathen king. Still, he was able not to compromise his faith. The sixth chapter of Daniel tells us that 70 years later, Daniel still had the habit of praying constantly.

> *To lead in these times, to take soldiers, sailors, and airmen into battle, you will be required to have character, competence, and be uncompromising.*
> — *H. Norman Schwarzkopf*

It's a shame that we, who are used to an atmosphere of religious tolerance, get our feelings hurt when someone expresses derision of our faith. Our lives aren't in danger. How often do we compromise?

Ezekiel compares Daniel to Noah and Job (Ezek. 14:12). Daniel was still living at that time, yet his godliness was compared to those two great men, long dead. Job was one of the greatest men of the East, and Noah held up his standard against all the rest of the world. That kind of integrity is priceless.

Why did Nebuchadnezzar want to educate these young men? He intended to brainwash them to be loyal to him and to rule over the Jews for him. When you take someone who is young, you can usually mold them as you want to. It didn't work in this case.

Nebuchadnezzar intended to use luxury and his wealth to brainwash them. By giving them great material wealth, he hoped to obligate them to serve him. That can cause us to compromise. It happens today. Those who have high paying jobs with a lot of perks can feel pressured into compromising their ethics for the sake of the company's business. Money can be used to destroy people when they get their eyes on things.

> *It's all right to have things, as long as things don't have you.*
> — *Jim Agard*

Money won't buy happiness, but it does carry with it responsibility. Money, properly used, can be a blessing. Happiness only comes through Christ.

The four who stood strong were Daniel, Hananiah, Mishael, and Azariah. Out of the entire group, these four refused to compromise. Their stand carried a real risk, not just ridicule, but possibly their lives. Being excellent in God's presence requires taking a strong stand for Him.

The king even gave them new, Chaldean names instead of their Hebrew names. By changing their names from Hebrew to Chaldean, the king was giving them a different identity. They were pagan names. The new names all represented pagan deities. We know the others better as Shadrach, Meschah, and Abednego.

When you forget your identity in Christ, you'll begin to compromise your faith. You'll begin to act the way you did before you came to Christ. That's what Satan tries to do to us when he tries to get our minds full of pagan thoughts. He wants us to think pagan so we'll act pagan.

Don't lose your identity. Don't have an identity crisis. We're born from above, we're new creatures. The old man is no longer there, the new one is alive in Christ.

When we know that we're cleansed, why do we keep going back to our sin? Because we forget who we are. We're the King's kids! We're champions, we're winners, we're special. We're no longer lost sinners, we're redeemed. When we forget that, we're easily defeated.

Daniel received the new name, but he still refused to compromise and eat things which were forbidden by God. He refused to become defiled with things which had been offered to idols. He went to the official and told him that he didn't want to be contaminated with it. He didn't beat around the bush. He didn't lie and try to con his way out of it. There can seem to be a lot of reasons to compromise, but Daniel didn't do it.

Daniel had a clear conscience before God, which helped give him the strength he needed. He hadn't given to compromise in little things, so when a big thing presented itself, he had no precedent for justifying doing the wrong thing. You won't be able to stand against criticism if your conscience is convicting you about past actions.

Feelings won't maintain you. It takes logic and reason by the Holy Spirit to bring a real conviction, and to give you the ability to witness. Nothing will be able to move you. Stick with your conviction.

Experiences which cannot be backed up by

the Word of God will not keep you on the straight path. God wants you to think, not just to feel. The experiences will be there, but you need sound thinking to stay strong in the faith.

What would you do if someone placed a gun to your child's head and said, "Deny Christ or I'll kill him!" You wouldn't be able to withstand that kind of an attack unless you know who you are and know the destiny of that child. The saints in the Book of Revelation are saints because they overcame, and they overcame to the point of physical death.

The closer we get to God, the less temptation there is to compromise our testimony for the sake of physical safety. You realize that nothing they can do to your body really matters. They can kill the body, but not the spirit.

> *Faith can accept no compromise whatsoever.* — *Don Meares*

When we miss church to do secular things, we are compromising. Remember the movie *Chariots of Fire*? The hero had trained for the Olympics in the 100-meter event. When he found that it was to be run on Sunday, he refused to run, entering instead the much longer 400-meter event, which he hadn't trained for. God honored his principles and he won, setting a new world's record. Because he honored God and his conviction that Sunday was God's day, God miraculously honored him.

The story in Daniel tells us that they refused

to defile themselves by eating the king's meat, which had been offered to idols. They asked instead that they be allowed to eat just vegetables and water. When the official expressed his fear that they would become malnourished, Daniel asked for a short trial of his plan.

The Bible states that at the end of the 10-day trial, their appearance seemed better. They were fatter than all the youths who had been eating the king's choice food.

When you won't compromise, God will come on the scene. He'll intervene. We don't want to get fatter, but we do want God to intervene. He doesn't leave us to shift for ourselves when we stand fast for Him and refuse to compromise.

> Who is there to harm you if you prove zealous for what is good? Be intensely enthusiastic in doing good deeds, because most people will not persecute someone who is doing good works (1 Pet. 3:13;NKJV).

People have a hard time hating someone who is always doing something good for them. How can you hate someone who bakes you a cake? How can you be mad at someone who comes over and mows your lawn or pulls weeds for you? It's hard to stay mad at somebody who keeps loving you. (This idea can help a marriage.)

The exception to this might possibly happen, but the chances are much less. Some God-haters will not be deterred by good works, but most people respond kindly to someone who loves, cares, and helps.

Set a goal to live a high standard that will set you apart, and your life will shine for God in the community. People will respect you when you mean what you say, say what you mean, and act out what you believe.

We live in a world that is filled with the problems caused by compromise. Society treats the symptoms and not the real disease. Trying to cure the situation with rules alone is like putting a bandaid on a severed arm. If smoke fills the inside of your car, that smoke is only visible evidence that some problem exists.

Drugs, pornography, abortion, homosexuality, pre-marital sex, and the violence that pervades our world are only symptoms of the problem. The problem is a society that has rejected God, has rebelled against His law, and has lost all sense of moral values.

On a personal level, compromise can be started because of pressures, loneliness, rejection, and emptiness. A life without Christ can destroy a person just as surely as it can destroy a nation.

We can't go by circumstances, we have to go by God's Word. "Trust in the Lord with all thine heart; and lean not unto thine own understanding," says Proverbs 3:5. God is the only one we can really trust.

> *Secret number fourteen: Don't ever compromise your principles.*

Secret 15

FAITH — Change

Don't worry about what you can't change. You can't change your birthday, your ethnic roots, or the past. With God's help, you can change your future.

Faith can help bring an inner peace to you. It will help diffuse confusion. It will reduce a lot of hurt. It will stop the fighting and struggle process. It will bring healing and recovery, and God will see you through.

We can't change most of what we worry about anyway. We can change how we think about situations, our attitude, and aspects of our personality. Those things can be changed.

You can get your life out of the rut by changing the habits that created the rut; or you can allow your future to be determined by the ruts in your present.

With faith in God, you are not a failure. You're not hopelessly in trouble. You are an original, you are the best, you're wonderful, you're a choice person, you're number one, you're different, you're not inferior, you're special, you're one of a kind. Don't ever run yourself down. There are billions of people in the world, and no one is just like you. Your fingerprints are unique.

You can believe God. God made you, He loves you, He cares about you, He forgives you, He accepts you, and He wants to help you. Believe in who you are. Have faith in who you are and stop the worry about what you can't change. You can't look forward to the future when your mind is always dwelling on the past.

Paul said, "I can do all things through Christ which strengtheneth me" (Phil. 4:13). The Bible tells us to love our neighbor as ourself. How can I love my neighbor if I don't love myself? It's wrong not to love what God loves, and He loves you. It's not wrong to have good feelings about yourself.

Don't be your own worst enemy. Give yourself a jump start. Stand up, be somebody, do something with your future. Your future begins today.

> *Never go to sleep at night until you are sure you have done all God wanted you to do today. Once you close your eyes, this day is gone forever. — Carl Allen, breeder and racer of champion trotting horses*

Faith can help you succeed. It's how you look at and handle situations that can help you adapt to change. Don't seek success itself. Live and walk in faith, then success becomes the natural by-product.

Some mischievous kids put Limburger cheese on their grandfather's mustache. When he woke up, he said, "The room smells." He went into the next room and commented, " The whole house smells." As he went outside, his reaction was, "The whole world smells!" In reality, it was only his mustache.

We can be unstoppable if we decide. We were created to control circumstances with faith. Don't let your fear bring circumstances to control you.

Lick your troubles, or they will lick you. Refuse to dwell on the negative. In everything give thanks, whether things go right or wrong, whether we are treated badly or well or misunderstood, whether we are sick or in good health.

God will help us. We face the need, recognize it, and go on and believe God. We climb a ladder one rung at a time. We travel 10,000 miles, 1 mile at a time. You can swallow a watermelon one bite at a time.

Believing in God is the answer. It can change impossible situations. It can unlock doors of power. It'll hook you up to God. It'll help you go beyond your imaginations.

> *Real faith in God today will change your future for tomorrow.*
> *— Dan Gaub*

You say "I'm not going fast enough." Anything worth having is worth hanging in there and believing in. Everything takes some time: it takes nine months to have a baby. It takes that child about a year to learn to walk, and nearly 20 years to become a mature responsible adult. Change takes time.

No one will ever lose unless he loses faith in God. Great people are never stopped, they have joined the non-stoppers. When you have hope and patience and persistence, you will begin to recover and succeed and win. A person like this just can't be defeated.

> *Asking who ought to be the boss is like asking who ought to be the tenor in the quartet. Obviously, the man who can sing tenor.*
> *— Henry Ford*

Why do we have challenges? God is a God of good, but He allows things to happen for a reason. Originally, golf balls were smooth and shiny. When it became apparent that old, dented balls went farther and straighter, they began making them with dimples. Rough spots make you go farther, and bring out your best. Don't fear change.

You have an open door. No one can shut it, it's your choice. The past doesn't matter, where you've been or what you've done. It's where you're headed that counts.

With the wisdom and the insight and the dreams that God has given you, you can dare to go beyond where you've ever been before. You can overcome obstacles and challenges. You can travel the miles and climb the stairs. You can unlimit yourself and go for the impossibilities. You can make it happen. You can trade bad priorities for good ones.

Have faith in God. Believe that faith will trigger the power that God has put within you. It will give you the desire to make it through. It'll help you make the right kind of decision. It'll bring enthusiasm. I love people who have enthusiasm with their faith. David was his own cheerleader. He changed his attitude. Maybe you should write yourself a letter and cheer yourself up.

You'll have the joy. You'll have the acceptance of God. You can do it. An atheist can't find God for the same reason that a burglar can't find a policeman. Neither one is looking.

You have faith, and God will see you through. If you want to finish in faith, you have to start in faith. Proverbs 29:18 says that where there is no vision, the people perish.

If our faith is tested, we can make it through. Believe that faith puts you on the building crew, and keeps you off the wrecking crew. Faith will oil the hinges of your doors.

Faith will give you the ability to withstand a crisis and remain in charge of your behavior. Faith will help you have purpose and boldness. It will make you action oriented, and able to welcome changes.

> *Secret number fifteen: Don't be afraid to change.*

Secret 16

FAITH — Finances

I believe that God is getting a new crop of people ready, like those in the faith chapter (Heb. 11). They have purpose and boldness, They are action-oriented. They believe God. They have a different kind of thinking. Sometimes our thinking has to change. When I found out that God is supply-oriented by nature and not need-oriented, it totally changed my life. God is supply-oriented for you. Start believing that.

When my grandkids come to my house, they don't kneel down on the kitchen floor and beg for food. "Please, Papa, is it possible that we can eat? Can you work a miracle?" They don't do that — we have the food, they are my grandkids. When they come, they sit at the table and say, "I'll have a sandwich, please." They know I'm supply-oriented. God is supply-oriented.

When Jannessa, our oldest grandchild, was about four, she and I were hurrying through a mall. She asked me if we could get some ice cream. My first response was that we didn't have time. "But Papa, I really need some ice cream," she continued.

"Nobody really needs ice cream," I responded in adult fashion. "Besides, we just don't have time." She was quiet for a few minutes. Finally she said, "Papa, can I just tell you ONE thing?"

"Make it fast!"

"Actually, two things. In the event that there is time to get ice cream, I just want to say thank you and I love you very much," she smiled sweetly.

I guess you know that we found the time to go and get some ice cream! She totally manipulated my mind. She said "I love you."

God wants to hear "thank you" and "I love you" in advance. We can't "manipulate" God, but he wants to know we love him, not just with our words, but with our actions. He is supply-oriented. Whatever your need is, He has more than enough to take care of it.

Maybe you feel like a man who asked prayer for the sale of his house. He had come to the end of his rope. He said, "I don't know what else to do, I've been trying to sell my house for a year, I've done everything, and it won't sell. I finally gave up and took the sign down."

I said, "Don't give up. God will send you a buyer." He wrote his goal on a slip of paper, "God, help me sell my house." The very next morning someone knocked on the door asking if the house might be for sale. The house sold for its true value.

Satan has mind and soul termites that eat away at our hearts and minds. We can have a mental malignancy, and have problems believing. We need to believe what God's Word says. I never give up. We can believe. Jesus was our example. He had some heavy promotional things happen. He could have walked on a mud puddle, but He didn't do it, He walked on a lake during a storm. That's heavy promotion.

You will start saying, "God, I know that You are supply-oriented." God wants to meet your need almost more than you want it met. He has more than enough. You don't have to beg God to do something He already wants to do.

You can't be a tightwad with God. If you aren't generous with what you have, you will be tighter if you have more. He will never give you more than He can trust you with.

God has sometimes given me something which I really wanted. Then He has almost immediately asked me to pass it on to someone else who really needed it. Sometimes, I think that the bookkeeper up in heaven needs some help. Surely it would make more sense to eliminate me as middleman. But faith will help you obey God. He knows who He can trust.

Faith will help you overcome obstacles, It will help you major in the positive. It will help you live above circumstances. The martyrs mentioned in Hebrews 11 died terrible deaths. We are told that they were scourged, stoned, chained, and sawn in two. These must have been terrible deaths, but they all had a good report through faith (Heb. 11:35-39).

They lived above the circumstances. They remained calm and in charge of their behavior. They never gave up. Faith never gives up. Some people want an answer right now, and some people get an immediate answer. For others it may take some time. Real faith just never gives up.

These people turned negatives to positives, they zeroed in on the goal. Start thanking God now for the answer. God is a big God. You get what you believe for. Faith starts thanking God in advance.

True leadership must be for the benefit of the followers, not the enrichment of the leaders.

In 1992 the president of the United Way had a salary of nearly $500,000. He used funds from the organization to pay for trips to Europe on a Concorde airliner, as well as other extravagant perks. What a mess he made for United Way!

> *The best executive is the one who has sense enough to pick good men to do what he wants done and self-restraint enough to keep from meddling with them while they do it.* — *Theodore Roosevelt*

Non-profit organizations, ministries, and other charities should be above reproach, and should be careful that extravagance by their leaders and directors is discouraged. We should be good stewards of the things God trusts us with.

Past scandals in Congress have also pointed up this problem. More than 140 members of the House admitted to overdrafts. One of the 24 worst offenders admitted to bouncing over 700 checks with a total of almost $600,000. Another one bounced almost 1,000 checks. As the scandal broke, many decided to retire. Their lives were motivated by greed and are a lesson to all.

> *Leaders must be close enough to relate to their followers, but far enough ahead to motivate them.*
> *— John Maxwell*

Jesus taught us to be careful about stewardship. All ministries should be accountable to the people who support them. As people support us, these people also experience rough times. I want God to help me to be sensitive. The whole thing is really not just about money, but integrity. All donations need to be spent wisely. Gifts to ministries do more than pay bills, they touch lives.

By itself, money can't buy happiness, peace, or joy. Neither can living in poverty. Money is only the means to an end to meet our needs and bless others. Our attitude about money is very important. It is a gift or a loan from God and is not to be wasted.

We need financial goals and a plan to accomplish them. God told us to have dominion over the earth. When we are blessed financially, we honor God. I've had to face financial problems because of the way I did things in the past and my attitude toward finance. I would rather borrow than let anyone know we needed finances.

Debt can be a heavy burden. I've learned to hate debt with a passion. Debt seems to destroy us and enslave us. Debt can tear us apart. Credit can be all right if we understand it and manage it correctly.

To have financial freedom, you have to stay on course while working toward freedom from debt. Always be more concerned about repaying than borrowing. Your faith will bring rewards.

> *Most people who succeed in the face of seemingly impossible conditions, are people who simply don't know how to quit.*
> *— Robert Schuller*

Abraham Lincoln had 10 guidelines that many have adapted as their own. He followed them his entire life.

1. You can't be prosperous and discourage thrift.

2. You can't help small people by tearing down big people.

3. You can't strengthen the weak by weakening the strong.

4. You can't lift the wage earner by destroying the wage payer.

5. You can't help the poor by destroying the rich.

6. You can't keep out of trouble financially by spending more than your income.

7. You can't further the brotherhood of men by inciting hatred.

8. You can't establish security on borrowed money.

9. You can't build character and courage by taking away a person's initiative and independence.

10. You can't help others permanently by doing for them what they could and should do for themselves.

A leader is someone who has two characteristics. First, he's going somewhere; second, he's able to persuade someone else to go with him. If no one is following, he's just out for a walk.

> *Secret number sixteen: Believe that God is supply-oriented.*

Secret 17

FAITH — Through the Construction Area

The road to success in any endeavor is always under construction. Faith will help you get through the construction area.

> *The only person who can stop you*
> *from becoming a success, is you.*
> — *Connie Agard*

Often in a zone where the state is completely rebuilding a road, there will be a car or small truck carrying a sign which reads "PILOT VEHICLE, FOLLOW ME." As long as the traffic follows the vehicle, there are no problems. The driver knows what hazards to avoid, when it's safe to proceed, and when to wait for moving equipment.

> *The most pathetic person in the world is someone who has sight, but has no vision.*
> *— Helen Keller*

Faith is like that vehicle. As long as we follow the leading of the driver (God), and move as he directs, we arrive safely at the other end of the zone.

Faith is really needed for America, and our world. A high government official made the statement, "We're fighting for survival." Faith is needed to help us make it through.

The person who eventually succeeds is the one who uses a defeat or setback as an opportunity to check the plan and see what went astray. Every defeat has seeds of benefits. Before it can help you, you must overcome the tendency to be hindered by fear.

You should never accept defeat as something permanent which would curse you and prevent you from trying again. Failures can be temporary.

> *Absorb the principle that failure is never final. If you do not succeed the first time, keep on trying.*
> *— Daisy Osborne*

If you depend just on man, you only get what man can do. If you depend just on your education, you get the benefits of that education, and what it can give you. IF you depend on faith, you get what God can do.

Bulldog faith hangs on to God's Word until our enemy is defeated and our circumstances change.

Fear erases faith. You are redeemed property, you are delivered, you are loosed, you are set free. Talk victory, faith, and happiness.

Abraham had faith (Gen. 18:23). He interceded for Sodom. Moses had faith when he interceded for Israel (Exod. 32:20). Samuel had faith when he interceded for the king (1 Sam. 7:5). Jesus had faith for the entire world (Matt. 26).

> *God does not give victory over the world just to a select few, He has given overcoming victory to every person that is born again.*
> *— Billy Joe Daugherty*

Faith will affect every part of our lives. Let me remind you that faith affects our thoughts. They become words, words become actions, actions become habits, habits form our character, and our character becomes our destiny.

Faith should influence every part of our life positively.

There is a "big question" everywhere you go. In New York, it's how much money do you make? In Philadelphia, who's your family? In Detroit, what car do you drive? In Washington, DC, do you work for the government? In Boston, what school did you graduate from? In L.A., who do you know in Hollywood?

But a larger question is, how is faith working in your life?

> *The nose of the bulldog has been slanted backwards so he can breathe without letting go.*
> — *Winston Churchill*

It's really amazing what you can accomplish when you have the faith to do it.

You're as young as your faith, and as old as your fears; as young as your confidence, as old as your doubts; as young as your dreams, as old as your despair.

You can believe against all impossibilities. Faith has three things: imagination, organized planning, and persistence.

> *Great victories come out of great battles.*
> — *Smith Wigglesworth*

Problems are opportunities with a few thorns on them. Faith is believing the invisible. It's easy to believe what you can see. Faith helps you believe what you cannot see. It's the only force that can take the invisible and cause it to become visible.

> *Secret number seventeen: Follow the "Pilot Car" through the construction zone.*

Secret 18

FAITH — That Moves God

> Need does not move God, faith does. Vain repetitions do not move God, faith does. Much speaking does not move God, faith does.
> — Charles Capps

There is no real success in life without some kind of sacrifice made. Faith is not just trying to believe something, regardless of the evidence; but daring to do something regardless of the consequence.

This chapter consists of the personal testimonies of people who have experienced the moving of God through faith.

ONE CHANCE IN A BILLION

One afternoon while lifting a paint compressor, I badly strained my lower back and was unable to move without extreme pain. I asked some in the congregation to pray for me, but did not see immediate results. In fact, for about two weeks, I continued to suffer.

At a minister's retreat, a fellow pastor asked me why I didn't have the ministers pray for me. My response was that if I sent an order in for *World Book Encyclopedia* (which I was selling at the time), and it didn't arrive the next day, I wouldn't send in another order.

"You have more faith than I do," he told me.

The following morning, I woke up with no pain, completely healed. Since then, God has used me to pray for others with back problems and they have also been healed.

Another time, my wife and I were visiting Korea. My neighbor had asked me to call her son who was stationed there. She did not have his phone number, only a San Francisco APO address.

After checking into our hotel, I went down to the lobby to use the pay phone. Five of us were standing in line to use it. My mind was racing, "I wonder what coins it takes, will the operator speak English, what base should I ask for?"

As the man ahead of me reached the phone, I watched as he deposited the coins. One question answered.

Then I overheard him ask to speak to Rodney Funakoshi.

"I wish you were calling Rodney Funasaki," I remarked while he waited for his party to come to the phone.

He answered, "That could be his name."

Rodney came to the phone, and he asked, "Hey, is your name Funakoshi or Funasaki?"

"Rodney Funasaki," came his answer.

The man holding the phone said, "There is someone here from Hawaii who wants to talk to you."

He handed me the phone, and I was able to relay his mother's greeting in a miraculous way.

Woodrow Yasuhara
District Superintendent
Hawaii Assemblies of God

FAITH KEEPS PRODUCING

In 1956 a handful of believers met in my home. We felt that God was speaking to us to establish a new church on the north side of Fort Wayne. As we prayed and fellowshipped together, we felt that He would raise up a great church.

Over the intervening years, we have continued to trust the Lord and to stand upon his promises. I remember vividly the struggles as we met in a lodge hall, a community center, an Edsel dealership, the YMCA, a theater, and finally a small building on five acres of land. God added His blessing, and sent us new families.

A bus ministry was started. We began a "School of the Bible." We worked and we prayed. God sent in a faithful staff as we continued to grow.

The Lord honored our faith and hard work. Calvary Temple is now the largest evangelical church in the entire area. Over 100 missionaries attend our annual "Congress for World Missions." We have begun satellite churches throughout the entire area.

I have never doubted that the vision the Lord gave me when we first started the church would be fulfilled. He has honored our faith, and has done far beyond anything we could expect.

Dr. Paul E. Paino
Calvary Temple
Fort Wayne, IN

DON'T QUESTION GOD

When our son, Curtis, was five years old (1964), he underwent surgery for a brain tumor. We were told that at most he probably had one year to live.

During that year, there were spiritual battles, but Curt not only lived, he grew rapidly better. Several brain scans and MRI's showed that the tumor had completely disappeared.

Curt finished high school, and went on to graduate from Christ for the Nations in Dallas, Texas. He then returned home to become one of my associate pastors, and a close confidante.

In 1988, Curt began having symptoms of more problems, and an MRI showed that four tumors now existed. Since the doctors felt that operating would probably curtail many of his activities, we decided to do nothing. In July of 1993, surgery became an absolute necessity. The doctors felt that two of the tumors could probably be removed, and that the other two were inoperable. People of faith may feel fear, but they just conquer it.

After the operation, the doctor came to us with the good news that he had been able to remove all four. Curt then began the mending process.

In turning him in bed, a nurse dislodged a breathing tube, and was unable to get it reinserted into his trachea. Instead, it inflated his entire chest cavity and he nearly died.

He did manage to live through it, but no longer had any use of his limbs. I'm sure that he simply said in his heart, "Lord, I've fought long enough. I don't want to live like this. Just let me come home with You." A few days earlier he had remarked to his sisters, "What's so wrong with going to heaven?"

I firmly believe that if his faith had held, and everything else been in total alignment, he would still be with us. Faith in God's Word is more powerful than any other force in the universe. His homegoing in August of 1993 was triumphant for him, but seemed like such a loss to us.

We still rejoice in the 34 years that we had him. We also rejoice in the triumph over the first brain tumor when he was five. We also rejoice in the triumph of his faith over the four brain tumors.

> *Faith does not strain God, it honors Him. — Don Lyon*

We leave the rest in God's hands. I continue to preach faith, and to believe God's Word is forever true. Faith turns clouds into showers of blessing.

Don Lyon
Faith Center
Rockford, IL

NEVER SAY "NEVER"

For a number of years, I traveled the country speaking in public high schools on the subject of "Real Love." From 1980 to 1990, I spoke in over 1,700 schools to 1.6 million students. Not all administrators welcomed me with open arms. Most did, but not all. One principal told me, "You'll NEVER speak in this high school!"

I don't give up easily, and telling me "NEVER" was issuing a challenge. As my associate and I headed toward the exit, an idea struck.

We went quickly to the nearest K-Mart and purchased a bull horn. We returned to the vicinity of the school, where we stopped at a convenience store where a group of teens were "hanging out" and doing drugs. These kids were not exactly on the "Dean's List," unless it was his list of problems.

"Attention," I yelled over my bull horn. The teens thought I was the LAW, so I had their attention. No one moved. "I'm a youth counselor from Tacoma, and I'm writing a book. I need some input. I'll be back tomorrow about noon. Be here if you've got the guts!" I closed the van door, and we left.

The next day at noon we returned to the store. Instead of just a few kids, about 200 were there. I left the van and plunged into the middle of them, calling questions with my bull horn, and recording their shouted answers on my tape recorder.

After about 20 minutes, as I started to leave, one young man shouted, "Hey, man, we've told you how we feel. You tell us how you feel."

"Okay," I said. "You go tell the principal that you want me to speak to the student body, and I'll tell you how I feel about these things."

As we drove away, we could see this entire group marching toward the school. When I reached my motel a few minutes later, the red light was blinking on the telephone. I picked it up and the operator informed me that the principal was holding for me.

"Mr. Wilkerson, would you please address our student body tomorrow morning at 8:30? I have 200 of our worst problem students staging a sit-in in my office." He was nearly begging.

"Well," I hedged, "10:30 would be better for me."

"You've got it!" he said as he hung up.

The next morning I had the privilege of speaking for an hour to the entire student body, and was thanked by the same principal who had said, "Never!"

You should never say never to God.

Rich Wilkerson
Tacoma, WA

> *Secret number eighteen: Faith will move God to perform miracles in your life.*

Secret 19

FAITH — Your Goals

You can't reach a goal until you decide what that goal is. You must have goals. It's important that we exercise real faith in God, not just have faith in faith. If you have no goals, it's absolutely sure that you won't reach any.

Some preachers preach against faith and positive living and even teach poverty, yet they move to another pastorate where they will have a larger salary. God wants all His children to be blessed financially. You can't possess too much money. If the money possesses you, any amount is too much.

Much has been written about setting goals. We continue to learn. (My book, *Dreams, Plans, Goals,* has a large section on reaching goals.)

> *There are no victories at bargain prices. — Dwight D. Eisenhower*

Most of us are told quite young not to dream, but to be realistic. Commitment to a dream doesn't close doors, it opens them. Following your dreams doesn't mean ditching responsibilities. Don't throw your dreams away, thus losing the success you could have had.

We must first make our goals solid, serious, and put some deadlines on them.

To reach a specific goal, you need a workable plan, and a dream to follow. What do you want to achieve? What other goals have you already reached? You need clear vision and accurate thinking, as well as a lot of determination. Look at the pattern.

Write your goal down. Say it out loud to yourself at least once a day. See it in your mind as being accomplished. It should make you excited. If you aren't excited about something, you won't excite anyone else about it.

We should be willing to make changes in order to reach the goals we are believing for. We need to stay excited, to establish a positive attitude around us. Think like a millionaire. Think like successful people. Think like those who are doing something.

Don't tell me something doesn't work if you haven't tried it. You say, "I'm hanging on by a thread" — take your threads and turn them into a rope.

Some people want to tell you how to invest money, but they haven't done very well with their own. How can they help you with yours?

Don't take advice on growing hair from a bald man. Don't take advice on weight loss from someone who is very overweight. Don't take advice on money from someone who is "broke."

> *Don't confuse fame with success; Madonna is one, Helen Keller is the other. — Erma Bombeck*

God put our eyes in the front of our heads so that we can go forward. Faith makes us go forward. Don't confuse activity with accomplishments.

I love to fly. Most of my more than six million miles are on United Airlines. I can tell you that airplanes aren't built to sit on runways, they are built to fly. You were not created by God to have no goals in your life. You were created by God to move.

"Everything you have ever learned got you to where you are now. We will all end up in life in direct correlation with who we listen to, the books we read, and the people we associate with," states Charlie "Tremendous" Jones.

We need to start focusing on how strong our faith is, not how tough things are, and how things won't work. We need mustard seed faith. There's nothing like mustard seed faith — a bird eats the seed, he digests it and it passes through, falls to the ground, the rains come, and a little tree comes up from the seed.

My good friend, Jim Agard has said many times that success will never attack you. It's not going to sneak up on you while you sleep. If you want success in reaching your goals, you have to attack them.

People are taught to not have faith, but to worry. When you tell them some challenge, they say, "I'd worry if I were you," or "Don't get your hopes up." We need to get our hopes up.

No matter how many successes you have attained so far in your life, the world is changing.

> *Goal-setting is a very important activity that separates the achievers from those who are just "getting by." — Connie Agard*

The world is changing faster than ever. Sometimes the old traditional methods have become rigid and inflexible and will not work for some people. We believe goal setting is important and should be based upon the Bible.

You need to set up an obstacle check list so you can check the things that are hindering you from reaching your goals. Otherwise you could be left behind in the world of change. You may not reach your goals because you will be distracted by circumstances.

With a check list, you can check your goals each day in just seconds. You can see how you are doing and what you need to do to become more activated in reaching your goals.

You want to make the most of your energy, of your time, and the potential that God has given you. You want to overcome the many pitfalls in a changing world. You can be on the cutting edge of achieving goals in today's world. Your life can thrive and be blessed in the challenges that you face under any circumstance.

> *Some set goals in the past on a long-range basis and didn't see immediate results so they became cynical.*
> *— Dave Williams*

Long-term goals and short-term goals need to be set. Good times or bad times, it doesn't matter. Set goals now.

It doesn't really make any difference if we run into challenges. Some people think that means they are out of the will of God.

If you look at the life of Paul, he was shipwrecked. He was in a storm, and the ship broke up. Most people would have quit, but not Paul. He got all wet, but he had a plan and a goal. He got bitten by a snake, but he shook it off and went about his business.

"Where there is no vision, the people perish," (Prov. 29:18) but there is a world of opportunities available for anyone who has a vision.

> *On the plains of hesitation bleach
> the bones of countless millions who,
> at the dawn of victory, sat down to
> wait, and waiting — died.*
> *— George W. Cecil*

Your rewards in life are in direct proportion to the service that you put out. Don't just drift through life — have a definite purpose. It is a starting point. It can also be a stumbling block for many people, because they don't define their goals, they just drift through life.

Only a small percentage really want to have success, and have definite goals and faith to reach those goals. They have a determination to get there. Realize that God wants you to have the desires of your heart.

> For the eyes of the Lord run to and fro throughout the whole earth, to shew himself strong in behalf of them whose heart is perfect toward him (2 Chron. 16:9).

> Fear not, little flock; for it is your Father's good pleasure to give you the kingdom (Luke 12:32).

Things that keep us from reaching goals:

Lack of self-discipline
Lack of self-improvement

Lack of ambition
Lack of persistence
Lack of good mental attitude
Lack of motivation
Lack of vision
Lack of imagination
Listening to negative people
Unwillingness to go the extra
mile.

> *When you get right down to it, one of the most important tasks of a leader is to eliminate his people's excuse for failure.*
> — *Robert Townsend*

A person who seems to fail but continues to fight usually discovers a source of creative vision inside himself. This enables him to convert a temporary defeat into a permanent success.

Do you realize that God cannot help you if you do not make up your mind what you want and where you want to go?

Your Father knoweth what things ye have need of, before ye ask him (Matt. 6:8).

We talked about the mind in chapter three, which has been made to receive and attract what it needs, just as a magnet will attract iron filings. The most difficult part of anything is getting started, moving on the goal that you want to achieve.

What you know isn't nearly as important as what you do with what you know.

Decision — desire — determination — discipline — direction — all are very important.

Avoid daydreaming — TV — self-pity — complainers — negative people — these will tear you down.

Be around people who can bring out the best in you.

Just as faith without works is dead, so works without faith is usually fruitless.

People who are most effective in reaching their goals use all the knowledge available to them. You may not think you need to make graphs and charts, but it will be worth the effort.

The one most important factor you should never forget about reaching a goal is to have one. You can't reach goals if you don't have any.

If you aren't willing to pay the price for success, you will pay the price for failure.

> *Secret number nineteen: Set goals*
> *and move toward them.*

Secret 20

FAITH —
Finishing the Race

Remember, you can't arrive at the finish unless you make the trip. This applies not only to our life as a whole, but to each thing we set out to do.

We pray for our finances, our businesses, our families, our friends, our church, our future. Many times the circumstances don't change like we want them to and we have a tendency to give up. If the circumstances don't change, God gives supernatural power to go through or around or over the circumstances.

We will see the stabilizing that God wants us to have. Faith stands or is sustained by grace. It's His grace, the favor from God, that helps us stand when we're standing in faith. Some have the tendency to become material-prone in this area. You pray for God to deliver you financially. If the money comes through, we have the tendency to trust in that money, even though we got it by faith. Your faith is not standing because of what it brings into existence, it's standing because of grace.

If it wasn't that way, God wouldn't have told us not to trust in riches. He would have said if your faith can bring you the riches, go ahead and trust them, but He said not to do that. He knows there are times Satan will come in and bring accusations against us.

Sometimes the accusations are true, usually not, but it opens a doorway where we can be buffeted. Satan wants to oppress us and come against us with all his might, trying to hijack our lives. He does that to get more access to us, which either prevents or slows down a miracle from coming.

We've got to know how to stand, even when the circumstances are not changing. We must trust and believe that God will come through and rescue us. Let's look at how people stand in times of crisis so that we can take those principles and apply them to ourselves.

We must be able to stand, even when the circumstances are not on our side. We need a bold tenacity to be unmoved by what we see or feel. We can't always trust our emotions.

We must be able to stand firm until God brings it to pass. Even in the worst possible adversity, we must stand. There is no such thing as a hopeless situation, only people who grow hopeless about a situation.

God will reward those who stand, no matter how hard it seems on our spirits. We simply need to do what He says.

People take verses that project only material victories and earthly things. That could be dangerous. Because Satan is the accuser of the brethren, God does allow him to come in at times and buffet us. We're still winners and champions.

Satan sometimes is allowed to overcome the visible Church in some way of physical or material captivity. You can still have surviving faith, even if it means going as far as martyrdom.

Satan was given authority for a certain period of time. Does that mean that the Church didn't overcome spiritually? Revelation 12:11 says, "They overcame him by the blood of the Lamb, and by the word of their testimony; and they loved not their lives unto the death." They were not willing to deny the Lord Jesus Christ, so even though some died, the Church triumphed spiritually. That's victory. Martyrs for Him will receive a special blessing for having endured such suffering. They finished their race.

Even though we sometimes have battles to fight, we always come out the winner in Him. Even the martyrs for Him died in victory (see Heb. 11:36-39).

> Let us hold fast the profession of [our] faith without wavering; (for he [is] faithful that promised;) And let us consider one another to provoke unto love and to good works: Not forsaking the assembling of ourselves together, as the manner of some [is];

but exhorting [one another]: and so much the more, as ye see the day approaching (Heb. 10:23-25).

Several things will help stabilize your faith so that you can finish the race. One of these is fellowship. This is a necessary thing, especially in times of tribulation. Hebrews was probably written a few years before the destruction of the temple in Jerusalem, but not before times had begun to get rough for the believers.

God knew that, so He gave them special instructions. He taught them how to prepare for perilous times. As you see these things happening, do the things commanded in the verses.

> *Have you completed today's mission in faith that God called you to do?* — *Chet Allen*

Hold fast to the confession of our hope without wavering, a continual act of consistency. We don't have to waver, we can consistently follow the things of God. In order not to waver, you have to do what God's Word says. You can't pick and choose what's popular for the time, you've got to do all of it.

Jesus said in His Word that we would waver back and forth. Some people will fall for everything, because they don't stand for anything.

Here's one of the things that will keep you from wavering: Let us consider how to stimulate one another to love and good deeds. Consider it, consistently, not just on Christmas or Easter, but all the time.

You can tell when the bond of fellowship starts to break down with a friend or in a church this way. You won't see as many people stimulating each other to love and good deeds. The devil can get us so busy making money and succeeding at careers that we don't have time for fellowship, or friendship or to invest in one another. Statistics indicate that 83 percent of those who attend church, attend a specific church because of friendships.

All we are consumed with is accomplishing our goals. This is one of Satan's tools so that when perilous times come, we fall. I have friends who call me often, and I call them. Every week, pastor friends from somewhere in the world will call me just to talk for a few minutes. It always touches my heart when someone cares enough to call and keep a friendship going.

There are others who are always too busy for fellowship, and so our friendship doesn't flourish as it should. Friendship is a two-way street, and both sides need to work to keep the friendship strong. If it's only one-sided, it will soon fall apart.

The American church is lacking in fellowship. A lot of churches have tried home fellowships, and they cut out a worship service to have the home fellowship and think they've mastered it. They're cutting back. We don't need to cut back, we need to add to. We need both home fellowships and the church services.

People complain about going to church two

or three times a week. It's impossible to raise your kids in this day and age with just a single 30 to 45-minute sermon per week. They need to get connected with kids in a youth group, and to make the right kind of friends. They need to be taught personally by a youth leader. They need time invested in them. They need fellowship if they are going to finish the race.

We need to come together, and not just to fill up seats. We need it to stay sustained by the grace of God. When someone knows you, they can sense when you're down and troubled, and can encourage you. Our friend Virginia Nordberg calls to see how we are. No matter what we say, she seems to sense exactly how we really are.

Our prayers are most effective toward those that we are closest to because we can believe with our whole heart. A stranger is different, but we usually care about those we know. We need corporate power — fellowship in the church and with one another.

It's not a sin to miss church, but it is a sin to consistently miss the services of the church when it is possible to attend. We must find time for God or we'll fall apart when truly perilous times come. Church should be a priority in our lives both as a family and on a personal level.

We need to be involved in and responsible to a local church. Without this kind of involvement, there is no accountability. There is no "storehouse" to collect and dispense the tithe. The work of the church suffers in missions, alms, and other ministries. We need the support of each other in order to finish the race well.

Paul wrote, "I speak to you according to the grace of God given unto me that ye think not more highly of yourself than you ought to but according to the measure of faith that God has dealt with you" (Rom. 12:3;NKJV).

Always remember this, whatever position you're in, whatever you're doing, no matter how prosperous you are, remember that it's all by His grace.

Some people use God's grace to its utmost. Other people don't use God's grace. They're lazy and they're having problems because they just don't use the opportunities that God gives them. Others don't make good use of the opportunities God gives them.

Don't think that faith is only about finances. Let me use this example. Why does one person bring in a million dollars a year, while the best someone else can do is twenty thousand? God's grace does not always give equal opportunities. God knows who can be trusted. God never gives us more than He can trust us with. I have never really liked to hear this, but I believe that it's true.

One person is smarter than another because God makes one brain smarter than the other. It's grace. And when you see that, it makes you realize that you are what you are because of the grace of God. Paul said he worked harder than anyone else, but that it wasn't him, it was the grace of God working in him.

God doesn't seem to give everyone the same opportunities, but everyone is just as precious in his sight. God has called the foolish things of this earth to shame the wise and the weak things to shame the strong.

Job lost everything, but he said God gives, and God takes away. He realized that it was grace. His friends told him that bad things don't happen to good people. But God told him that wasn't true. In the end, because Job stayed true to God, he prospered financially with twice as much as before.

If you're doing everything you're supposed to do, remember that it's God's grace that allows you to do anything. This keeps your perspective true. Let's keep our spirit humble before Him, as we finish our race.

Secret number twenty: Keep your eyes on the goal, and move ahead. You'll finish in victory.

This book of the law shall not depart out of thy mouth; but thou shalt meditate therein day and night, that thou mayest observe to do according to all that is written therein: for then thou shalt make thy way prosperous, and then thou shalt have good success (Josh. 1:8).

FINAL NOTES

We are either moving forward in our lives, or we are moving backward. Here is a list to help you measure your progress.

1. Am I where God wants me?

2. Am I using my talents to their full potential?

3. Am I fair to others?

4. Am I guilty of offending others by my words or actions? If so, do I correct it?

5. Am I striving to make positive changes in my life?

6. Has my attitude been right toward those I live and work with?

7. Have I personally improved? How?

8. Have I made right decisions? If not, have I corrected them?

9. Is the quality of my work something that I can feel good about?

10. Do I encourage and build up people so that they feel better after being with me?

11. Do I treat others the way I would like to be treated? What can I change?

12. Am I thankful or do I take others for granted?

13. Am I considered a "dreamer"? If not, why not?

14. Have I reached my top five goals in the last year? If not, what changes do I need to make so that I can?

If you would like to write Ken Gaub and have him speak in your area, he can be contacted through:

Ken Gaub Worldwide Ministries
P.O. Box 1
Yakima, WA 98907 USA
(509) 575-1965
FAX (509) 575-4732

• Other books by Ken Gaub •

Available at Christian bookstores nationwide

Answers to Questions You've Always Wanted to Ask
0-89221-207-1
144 pages

Dreams, Plans, Goals
0-89221-244-6
144 pages

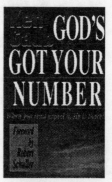

God's Got Your Number
0-89221-211-X
160 pages